CANDLES FOR ADVENT

Pauline Webb is a broadcaster and writer who lives in Wembley, northwest London, where in fact she was born. But her home could more accurately be described as the "world-house" of the ecumenical movement. Throughout her life she has travelled extensively, first as the daughter of an itinerant Methodist minister, and in her adult life through her own commitments in the worldwide Church.

She worked for many years as editor of the Methodist Church Overseas Division, and later as its Secretary for the Caribbean and Latin America. More recently she has been the Organiser of Religious Broadcasting in the BBC's World Service. Since her retirement in 1987 she has continued as a regular contributor in Radio 2's "Pause for Thought" and to Radio 4's "Thought for the Day" and the Daily Service. She was also the presenter of a special international Advent series of "Songs of Praise" for BBC Television.

A former Vice-President of the Methodist Conference, she was elected Vice-Moderator of the World Council of Churches from 1968 to 1975, and chaired the committee responsible for planning the WCC's Sixth Assembly held at Vancouver in 1983, where she was invited to preach the opening sermon.

A Fellow of King's College, London, she holds degrees in English from London University and in Theology from Union Theological Seminary, New York. She has been awarded honorary doctorates from Universities in Brussels, Toronto and Halifax, Nova Scotia, in recognition of her contribution to promoting the role of women in the Church, combating racism and working for Christian unity and for inter-faith dialogue.

Candles for Advent

PAULINE WEBB

Collins
FOUNT PAPERBACKS

First published in Great Britain by
Fount Paperbacks, London in 1989

Printed and bound in Great Britain by
William Collins Sons & Co. Ltd, Glasgow

CONTENTS

The holly and the ivy
Are dancing in a ring
Round the berry-bright red candles
And the white and shining king.

Oh, one is for God's people
In every age and day.
We are watching for His coming.
We believe and we obey.

And two is for the prophets,
And for the light they bring.
They are candles in the darkness,
All alight for Christ the King.

And three for John the Baptist.
He calls on us to sing:
"O prepare the way for Jesus Christ,
He is coming, Christ the King."

And four for Mother Mary.
"I cannot see the way,
But You promise me a baby.
I believe You, I obey."

And Christ is in the centre,
For this is His birthday,
With the shining lights of Christmas
Singing: "He has come today."

EMILY CHISHOLM (1910–)

INTRODUCTION

A circle of light, glowing from candles mounted on an evergreen wreath, once heralded the return of the sun on the shortest day in the dark midwinter of the northern hemisphere. That was long before the winter solstice was decreed to be the appropriate date for the celebration of Christmas, the birthday of the one who would be heralded as the "Sun of Righteousness", bringing light and life to all the world.

The earliest mention of Advent itself as a season observed by Christians is in fourth-century Spain, where it is recorded that a three week period of fasting was kept leading up to the Feast of the Epiphany. It was in the time of Pope Gregory the Great that it was finally determined that the four Sundays preceding 25th December should be a time both of preparation for the Feast of the Nativity and of penitence at the beginning of a new cycle of the Christian calendar. During the period of Advent, which literally means "Coming", Christians were to ponder not only on the beginning of the Christian story but on its ending too, fixing their minds on both the first and the final coming of Christ into the world.

So Advent is not simply a countdown to Christmas. At a time when commercial pressures are constantly reminding consumers how many shopping days are left, and kitchens are busy with the preparation of puddings and cakes, the Church calls its people to a period of quieter reckoning, reflecting on the more lasting values of their lives and making themselves ready for the time when all things will be summed up in Christ at the final judgement.

The lighting of candles on an evergreen wreath, like so many other traditional customs, was eventually seen to have appropriate symbolism for the Christian observance. For many centuries it seems to have been a neglected ritual, but it emerged again in East Germany in the Middle Ages and became widespread in both Catholic and Protestant communities throughout Europe. During the twentieth century it has become a popular custom across the world. In 1896 Archbishop Nathan Söderblom, the Swedish ecumenical leader, commended the custom of lighting Advent candles in a sermon he preached in Paris, and this probably sparked off the rapid adoption of the practice elsewhere than in Scandinavia, where light has always been one of the most familiar symbols associated with the Christmas season.

The four candles for the Sundays of Advent, surrounding the fifth candle, which is lit on Christmas Day itself, point people to ways of preparing for the royal coming. There is some variation in the interpretation given to the four candles. In many churches, they are linked with the people who figure in the lessons appointed to be read on the appropriate Sundays. Thus, on the first Sunday the candle represents the People of God as they awaited the coming of the Messiah, and especially the Christian community as they anticipated the second coming of

Christ. On the second Sunday the candle commemorates the prophets who foretold the coming of the Prince of Peace. On the third Sunday, attention is focused on John the Baptist, the preacher who came to prepare the way of the Lord. The fourth candle is for Mary, the expectant mother, awaiting with mingled anticipation and apprehension the birth of her firstborn. Then on Christmas Day the candle is lit for Christ Himself, who came to bring light to all the world.

In other traditions, the Advent candles are associated with gifts of the Spirit rather than with particular people. The first Sunday is the Sunday of hope, the second of peace, the third of joy, the fourth of love. It is common practice in all traditions to observe the second Sunday in Advent as Bible Sunday, particularly relating to the collect for the day, and the third as "Laetare" day, the day of rejoicing, echoing the opening words of the epistle, "Rejoice in the Lord always".

There is some variation too in the colours associated with the Advent wreath. Since the twelfth century various colours have been introduced to mark the different seasons of the Christian year. Until that time, the liturgical colour was always white, but then began the custom of using red vestments at Pentecost and later at other great feast days. Then purple, the colour of penitence, became associated with the period of Lent, and, since it was also the colour of royalty, it became the colour of Advent too, as the Church prepares for the coming of the King. In recent years, some churches have chosen to distinguish between

Lent and Advent by adopting blue for the latter, the colour of hope, a dominant Advent theme. These variations are reflected in the choice of colour for the Advent candles. Some use white for the four Sundays and red for the festal candle of Christmas. Others have red for the surrounding candles and white for the central one. Some light purple or blue candles, and may mark especially the third Sunday with rose-pink, the colour of joy. The base of the wreath is usually made of wire, covered with evergreen, its circular shape intended to represent the unending, eternal love of God. It may equally well be carved of wood or made of metal or ceramic, and can be designed also to represent the world into which the light of Christ comes.

In this book, meditations on the passages of Scripture associated with each of the candles on the Advent wreath are interwoven with stories of people in different parts of today's world who personify the Advent themes. It is suggested that the candles are lit in a simple ceremony in the home or in church when the Advent passages are read, and that prayers be offered for the people whose stories are told here and others like them throughout the world.

The circle begins with the people of God among whom I am most at home, the congregation of my own church in Harlesden, an inner-city area in northwest London. Then I recall people I met on my travels when I was presenting the special worldwide Advent series of BBC Television's programme "Songs of Praise", in which places as far apart as Harare in Zimbabwe and Vancouver in Canada were linked together by candles lit on the same Advent wreath. Soon after that, I was sent by the Churches' Action for Central America to Guatemala and Nicaragua, where we met many people, particularly of the Baptist tradition, who seemed to me in deed and in word to be truly preparing the way of the Lord. For Christmas Day itself I have recalled my own most memorable Christmas, spent some years ago in the jungle of northern Burma among the Khongsai people, who have remained in my heart and prayers ever since, through the years when Burma's frontiers were closed until the more recent events and unrest in that land.

I owe particular gratitude to my friends in Vancouver who encouraged me while I was writing this book during a term I spent as a visiting scholar at the University of British Columbia, and especially to Seok-Leng Khor, of the Vancouver School of Theology, who so cheerfully and skilfully helped me out in the typing of it. For them and for all the people whose stories are told here, and whose shining witness has illuminated my own pilgrimage, I light these candles for Advent.

Advent One

One is for God's people
In every age and day.
We are watching for His coming.
We believe and we obey.

THE PEOPLE OF GOD

It was 6.25 on a dark Sunday evening, the first Sunday in Advent. In the vestry of an inner-city church in north London, the lay leaders were waiting anxiously. The invited preacher for the evening service had not yet arrived. Everyone was wondering what we would do if he failed to turn up.

His name, billed in bold letters on the notice board, had attracted the largest congregation ever seen in that church. It was more than packed to the doors. People were waiting outside too, in the bitter cold. Inside, chairs filled the aisles and children perched on the window sills. They had all come to hear the man who has been described as one of the greatest orators of our time, both in the pulpit and on a political platform – the Rev. Jesse Jackson. He was on a brief visit to London, in the midst of his campaign for nomination as Presidential candidate in the USA. His schedule was tightly packed, but he had promised to take time out, if he could, to come to Harlesden to visit our predominantly black congregation. Now the minutes were ticking relentlessly away, and it looked doubtful whether he would make it at all. People knew he had expended enormous energy that afternoon addressing an Anti-Apartheid rally in Trafalgar Square, and there were rumours of an impending appointment with royalty. So we hardly dared hope that he would still remember the promise extracted from him to come to this less than smart neighbourhood and to give us a whole hour of his time.

Half-past six chimed and he had not arrived. The organist struck up some favourite hymns, and the leaders hoped that the Caribbean cultural tradition of a relaxed attitude to punctuality would keep the people patient for the time being. But the clock ticked ominously on, and still no preacher arrived. The resident minister went into the pulpit, wondering how to avoid letting the occasion become too great an anti-climax. At least the sense of expectancy gave an appropriate atmosphere for the evening's ceremony, the lighting of the first candle on the Advent wreath.

"We light this," he explained, "as part of our waiting, not just for the arrival of Jesse Jackson, but for the much more important coming of Jesus Himself, whose advent we shall celebrate in four weeks' time."

The Sunday School teacher in charge of the children lighting the candles made it last as long as she could – even the match seemed suspiciously difficult to strike. But no one was concentrating on the candle-lighting. Everyone's eyes were on the door, willing it to open and reveal the guest's arrival.

Then suddenly, just as the clock struck seven, there

he was. The promised visitor had come. The senior lay leader, overcome earlier by apprehension and now by embarrassment, hardly knew how to welcome him.

"Mr Jackson," she said in her soft Jamaican tones, "we had almost given up the hope of your coming at all. After all, we know you are often the guest of great people, even of princes and princesses, and we are only second-class citizens in this land. But now you have arrived among us and it does our heart good."

"Mary," he replied, "I have come here to meet my royal princess." And he picked up one of the smallest girls in the front row. Holding her in one arm and waving his well-worn Bible with the other, he declared, "Here she is, for it says in this book that you are all, even the smallest and humblest among you, a part of the royal priesthood. And always remember this, there are no second-class citizens in the Kingdom of God."

So, for that congregation, Advent began appropriately with the claiming of the great biblical titles of the People of God, titles that convey a sense of divinely-given destiny and human dignity which no power on earth must be allowed to deny. For the Children of Israel, the sense that they were a People particularly chosen by God because He loved them and wanted from them a response of love, had sustained them through centuries of their history, from the Exodus to the Exile. Their hope was founded not on their strength nor their status in the eyes of the nations, but simply on the fact that God loved them and had made them heirs of a promised Kingdom. The Promise still lay in the future, but the Providence of God had been experienced throughout the past. So their hope consisted of both memory and anticipation. The God who had enabled them to survive would also surely send a Saviour who would come to claim their Kingdom.

> For you are a people holy to the Lord your God: the Lord your God has chosen you to be a people for His own possession, out of all the peoples that are on the face of the earth. It was not because you were more in number than any other people that the Lord set His hand upon you and chose you, for you were the fewest of all peoples; but it is because the Lord loves you and is keeping the oath which He swore to your fathers that the Lord has brought you out with a mighty hand, and redeemed you from the hand of Pharaoh, King of Egypt. Know therefore that the Lord your God is God, the faithful God who keeps steadfast love and covenant with those who love Him and keep His commandments to a thousand generations (Deuteronomy 7:6–9).

So the People of God were strong in the confidence that God loved them and no defeat by other nations, no discrimination against them, no demeaning of their status in slavery or exile must be allowed to shake that confidence. Having learned what it meant to be loved unconditionally by God, they were expected to show that same kind of love not only to God but to one another and indeed to all people. But some soon forgot those commandments. They became neglectful of their religious duties and unjust in their social dealings. Some settled down comfortably to enjoy an immediate prosperity, measuring their values by those of neighbouring nations rather than keeping clear the vision of the coming Kingdom. And in every generation the prophets called them to repentance, constantly holding before them the Promise still to be fulfilled. Just as in the past God had sent His servants to rescue them from slavery, so in the future He would send His servant to redeem them from their sins and to usher in the Kingdom of justice and peace.

But the Messiah was a long time coming and many grew weary in the waiting. When Israel's strength as a nation was at its weakest and the power of Rome was dominating the world, it seemed for a time as though even the prophets were silent. But there remained among the people the faithful few, the "remnant" as they were called, or the "survivors" as they might equally aptly be described. Some of these faithful withdrew into the wilderness, to wait there in penitence and prayer, poring over the holy books to tell where and when the Messiah would appear. Others went about their daily work, patiently, piously, still pondering on the promises. Many of these were the poor, the humble, the meek who yearned for a Messiah who would one day usher in a new order and upturn the values of the world around them.

The gospel stories begin with glimpses of some of these faithful few. There is a young girl who knows by heart Hannah's prophecy that the Lord would "raise up the poor from the dust, to make them sit with princes and inherit a seat of honour" (1 Samuel 2:1–10; cf Luke 1:46–58). There is a loyal carpenter, torn between his strict observance of the law and the dictates of his own heart. There is an old woman who knows the prophecies through and through and is always in her place in the Temple, and an old man, devout and patient in prayer, longing to see the Messiah before his eyes close in death. All these people of God are there in the Advent story – awaiting the coming of the Lord.

They are there too, these Advent people, in that London inner-city church, watching and waiting for the coming of the Day of the Lord. I recognize among my friends there the counterparts of those gospel characters, the people whom God chose to prepare the way for the coming of His Son.

There is Mrs T, who reminds me so much of that old widow Anna, who, in Luke's account of the presentation of the Christ child in the Temple, became the first evangelist, sharing with her neighbours the joy of having seen the Lord. Mrs T is one of the few white members left in our congregation. She must have been there for many long years, since the days when it was a flourishing suburban church, full of missionary zeal. Then came the war and the bombs and the rebuilding, and the subsequent flight to the newer suburbs as local families moved out and the immigrants moved in. But Mrs T stayed, loyal to her church even as she watched it changing beyond all recognition. As familiar figures passed on or moved away, she would always be there in her same familiar place, praying that one day the empty seats around her would be filled again and that God would raise up new leaders to fill the vacant offices. Today her prayers have been abundantly answered as she is surrounded by new friends, people whom she loves and who love her with such warm affection that there seems no such thing as racial barriers or generation gaps. As she said to me one day, "We used to sing at our missionary meetings,

> "Coming, coming, yes they are,
> Coming, coming from afar"

and now they have come, from the Caribbean, and from Africa, and from Asia. How fortunate I am to have lived to see this day and to enjoy their company!"

Then there is Fred, our contemporary Simeon, whose enthusiasm for the things of the Kingdom has not dimmed during his eighty years, and whose religious commitment is matched only by his political zeal. He must be one of the most well-read members of the congregation, serving at the book stall, always ready to recommend a new publication or persuade someone to subscribe to a periodical, as he watches and waits, longing to see a new social order and the signs of the coming Kingdom.

We have our Joseph too, though his name happens to be Philip, a carpenter who came to this country from his home in Jamaica at a time when people were being urged to come here, to help meet Britain's need then for labour. He brought with him a simple, shining faith and a trust in God's word which has never been extinguished, not even by the gloom of unemployment or sickness or the struggle to instil in his children a respect for the law, even though at times it seems as though some of those who enforce the law show little respect for them.

And there is many a young Mum, for whom there has been no room when they most needed it, except a temporary bed-sit with a cot in which to lay their new-born child.

For these people, every Advent begins with a Festival of Hope, when we invite as a guest preacher to the church someone whose faith has been forged on an anvil of adversity of one kind or another. It may be someone who comes, as Jesse Jackson did, out of the Civil Rights struggle in the USA. It may be a speaker who keeps faith and hope alive in the face of discrimination and deprivation here in Britain. It may be a visitor who comes proclaiming that the *kairos*, the hour of judgement, is at hand in South Africa. It may be someone who brings words of hope even from the valley of the shadow of death where they have walked with AIDS sufferers or with drug addicts. At this season of the year we always look for someone to speak to us who is "down to earth" as the saying goes, for we are anticipating the celebration of the One Who "came down to earth from heaven". However dark the present scene may be, at Advent time we try to see the immediate moment in the light of our hope for the dawning of a new day.

The People of God were a travelling people. It began when Abraham set out, not knowing the destination of his journey, and continued through Israel's journeyings across Canaan. Then came his sons' long trek to Egypt in search of food, and the wanderings of the Children of Israel across the wilderness until they reached the Promised Land. From the very beginning, life for the People of God had been a constant pilgrimage, marked by many sacred resting-places, but with no abiding city. The image of this wandering, travelling company has remained in Sister Estelle's Advent song. Its chorus is among the many our congregation sings as they set off in coaches for outings from London on their own pilgrimage journeys to sacred places that have so much to teach about the history of the Faith of which we are heirs:

> "Moses, I know you're the man",
> The Lord said.
> "You're going to work out my plan",
> The Lord said.
> "Lead all the Israelites out of slavery,
> And I shall make them a wandering race
> Called the People of God."

So every day
We're on our way
For we're a travelling, wandering race
Called the People of God.

In the New Testament the People of God are still bidden to live as pilgrims ready for a journey that may begin at any time: "Let your loins be girded and your lamps burning", Jesus urges the disciples, echoing the words to the People of God waiting for the Passover. "In this manner you shall eat it: your loins girded, your sandals on your feet and your staff in your hand" (Exodus 12:11).

Christians were from the earliest times known as "The People of the Way", those who have no abiding city, but always seek the city which is to come. As early as the second century after Christ's coming, the author of a Letter to Diognetus, describing the life of the Church in those times, said of the early Christians, "They share all things as citizens and suffer all things as aliens. They look upon every foreign land as though it were their fatherland, and upon their fatherland as though it were a foreign land."

Both citizens and aliens – that is an appropriate way to describe how many people, who have come from overseas to live in Britain, feel in this country. For many of them, it was a great act of faith to leave the sun-blessed shores of their tropical homes and come to the rain-drenched streets of London. They had little idea of where they were coming to or what they would do here, but as one of them put it to me, "You can't live on sunshine, and we had heard legends of how the streets of this city were paved with gold." They had been taught that this was their motherland and they trusted in the Providence of God to guide them on their way.

It was a cold coming for many of them. Like the Holy Family, some discovered what it is like to arrive in a place where you are told too late that there is no room. For one African family in our congregation, that message came very late indeed. They had been here fifteen years, when they were summarily told they could stay no longer.

Ben had always hoped to travel. Back home in Ghana, as a Boy Scout, he had enjoyed the trekking and the camping and the sense of adventure. He was lucky enough as a young man to be chosen to come as a Scout representative to an international camp here in Britain. It seemed to him like a land of opportunity and hope. So he decided to settle here. With his excellent secondary school qualifications and his conscientious attitudes he was one of the fortunate ones who was able to get a job. He found work as a mechanic, married a wife, provided a home and began bringing up a family. The warmth of the fellowship they found in the local church compensated for the loss of contact with their family and friends back in Ghana.

Then the blow fell. From a faceless bureaucracy somewhere in the city came a deportation notice. The papers by which Ben had entered the country fifteen years before were not in order, and he and his family must leave forthwith. Faced with such a dilemma what could he do? He had no prospect of work in Ghana, no home to go to, no resources to draw upon except the one resource he had always relied on. He took it to the Lord in prayer. And his new extended family, the congregation of his church, joined in those prayers, with petitions not only to God but to the Government too.

The local minister sent all the details to the Home Office, making a special plea on the family's behalf. Ben's wife, Lydia, was pregnant with their fourth child. The third baby was ill and under the care of a London hospital. By a quirk of the new immigration laws, the two older children had the right to stay in Britain, having been born here, but the younger one and the unborn baby had no such rights. It was just before Christmas, and a spirit of compassion prevailed. There was a temporary suspension of the deportation order to permit the whole family to stay long enough for the birth of the child and the celebration of the Festival.

But then the blow fell again. The family were ordered to leave immediately. It was suggested to them that they could, if they wished, leave the two older children in care in Britain but the younger ones were technically aliens and must go back with their parents.

The minister and congregation continued to stand by them in a solidarity of prayer and protest, offering them sanctuary if needed in the church itself. The local Member of Parliament, himself a member of the church, took up the case with those powerful ones in whose hands the fate of that whole family rested. After months of pressure on the one hand and harassment on the other, we heard the good news. It came one bright summer day, in our church notices: "The deportation order has been withdrawn. Ben and Lydia and the children can stay among us." And the congregation responded, "The Lord hears our prayer. Thanks be to God."

The Advent hope is not only about immediate events, or the birth of a Baby in Bethlehem, a place where He was unwelcome and unwanted. It is also about the time when "He shall come again in glory," as the Church proclaims, "to judge both the quick and the dead." So the early Christians were also an expectant People, watching and waiting for the coming of the Lord.

This Second Advent would be very different from the First. At His first coming, only the faithful few and the angelic host in heaven had recognized Him as He slipped quietly into human history. But at His Second Coming, they believed, all eyes would behold Him, and angels would accompany Him as He came to sum up all history in His judgements from a mighty throne. The poetic visions of the Hebrew prophets were reflected in Jesus' own teaching, in Paul's Epistles and in the Revelation of St John the Divine.

They all point to a cataclysmic event which would mark the culmination of the whole creation, ending not in a whimper but in a blaze of glory.

No one could prophesy where or when this would all happen, but by New Testament Christians it was believed to be imminent. They lived in daily expectation of the Second Coming of Christ. So their lives took on a new perspective. Far from the advice to "live each day as though it were the first day of the rest of your life", which has become one of the trite sayings of modern times, they were a people who lived each day as though it were their last. The Lord was nigh and might come at any moment. So they sat lightly to secular affairs. There was no point in owning property or hoarding money or even building churches. All these things had only temporal significance. But the gifts of the Spirit, like faith and hope and love – these were to be cultivated, for these were the values of eternal life.

Such expectation did not make people passive, but became a spring for their energetic action. The vigilance of the early Christians gave a new urgency to the work they had to do, carrying out Christ's commands, preaching the Gospel, healing the sick, feeding the hungry, teaching the faithful. Paradoxically, because they believed that human history was coming to an end they played a stronger part in shaping that history. They had no fear of the rulers of earthly kingdoms, for they saw their power as limited and their empires as crumbling. The Christians even lost all fear of death, for death itself would be defeated in the final victory of Christ. And because it was Jesus

who they believed would come to be the Judge of all
the earth, they had no fear of that Last Judgement.
They knew Him as One who showed compassion, who
forgave sins and who would bless those peoples who in
His Name had cared for the poor and the homeless,
provided for the hungry and thirsty and visited the
invalid and the prisoner. In Christ's Second Advent,
as in His First, the poor would be exalted and the
mighty brought low. But the judgement was to be His
and His alone – He would settle all scores and avenge
all wrongs. So it was no longer necessary for human
beings to take vengeance into their own hands or to
pass judgement on others. "Pass no judgement before
the time," advised St Paul, "until the Lord comes."

But as the time went by, it seemed as though the
Lord tarried. Every now and then some explosive
event occurred which people saw as an omen of His
coming, but as one prophecy after another failed to
materialize they began to realize that it was impossible
ever to know the time and season of the End. If it were
to be the end of all time, how could it be placed within
time itself? So, at the end of the first century, Peter
writes in his Epistle:

Do not ignore this one fact, that with the Lord
one day is as a thousand years and a thousand
years as one day. The Lord is not slow about His
promise as some count slowness, but is forebear-
ing towards you, not wishing that any should
perish, but that all should reach repentance. But
the day of the Lord will come like a thief and then
the heavens will pass away with a loud noise and

the elements will be dissolved with fire, and the earth and the works that are upon it will be burned up (2 Peter 3:8–10).

Peter goes on to argue that this very delay of the End should increase in Christians the determination to live as people of a new age, both waiting for and hastening the coming of the Lord. The Christian life has always held that kind of tension between anticipating the Kingdom and realizing that it is already here. We look for the coming of Christ, but we celebrate that He has already come. "Thy Kingdom come", we pray daily, but we try to live by that Kingdom's values here and now. "Thy will be done on earth, as it is in heaven."

So the Advent hope is a twofold hope. It is a looking back to an event in history when God entered into human life, and a looking forward to that mystery beyond history when our lives will be taken up into the very life of God. And the One Who was there in that first Advent is the One we shall celebrate in the second – Jesus Christ, the same yesterday, today and forever. I confess I had a hard time writing that passage. My literal mind finds it difficult to make much of the scriptural language about the Lord coming in clouds of glory and riding a white horse at the head of the armies of heaven. But one thing I have learned from my West Indian friends is to read the Bible not only with the eyes of the mind but with the eyes of the heart. Poetic visions present few problems to them. They come from a history in which people whose earthly life was so often made wretched were sustained by a faith in heavenly glory, the glow of which has never faded for them. They love to sing of crowns and thrones and trumpets sounding from the very courts of heaven, for the language of heaven is to them like the language of home. Their eyes really do seem to have seen the glory of the coming of the Lord, and that glory transfigures their lives, shining through their prayers, their praises and even the round of their daily tasks.

Dolly, who now, rest her soul, is, I believe, safe in that heavenly Kingdom, spent all her earthly days in the basement kitchen of a large London hospital, cutting up carrots for the patients' diets. I once asked her if it didn't get tedious.

"Sometimes", she said, "I do find it wearisome. But then I think of that last Day of Judgement when the Lord will come and ask what I've done to feed the hungry and I'll have buckets and buckets of carrots to show Him, and I think He'll let me in!"

Those who scornfully write off such talk of heaven as "pie in the sky" have failed to understand how sustaining and even subversive such confidence in the future can be. The slaves who sang of the shoes in which they would walk all over God's heaven were in fact protesting against the prohibition of their wearing shoes on the plantations, from where they were determined to effect their escape, even if they had to do it on their bare feet. And the vision of chariots and angels coming to carry them home gave to people who had been herded like cattle in the holds of slave ships an indelible sense of their human dignity.

Such hope is rooted in a communal memory which radically affects the way people still read their Bibles today. I remember an occasion when we had gathered in a home for Bible Study, just at the time when the film *Roots* was being shown on television. It was Alex Haley's story of how he, a black American, went to trace his family's origins back to the tribal home of a chieftain in West Africa. It was at times a brutal and violent film, and the group began discussing whether they would allow their children to watch it. One of them said she thought it was better for them to forget the past, lest it embitter their children against those among whom they must now learn to live. But another replied adamantly, "No, we must let our kids see what we have survived, and how much blood and toil and tears and sweat have gone into making us a people and bringing us here. Then they will see how, out of cruel bondage, the Lord has led us, as he led the People of Israel into a promised land of freedom." We turned from that conversation to study our appointed passage in Galatians 5: "For freedom Christ has set us free; stand fast therefore and do not submit again to a yoke of slavery", words which in that context had a powerful literal ring.

It is not only past memory that brings Scripture to life. People who live in an increasingly violent society find themselves re-living at times the agony and the cruelty which the people of that first Advent knew when life was cheap and enmities were fierce; and they look with hope towards heaven, with its guarantee of life's eternal value and of the ultimate mercy of God.

It was on a recent Good Friday that many of our congregation became caught up in a tragedy enacted right on the threshold of the church. They had gathered on the steps to sing some of the great Passion hymns before setting off in a procession of witness to carry the cross through the streets of the city. A young man, who worked in a café opposite, joined them to sing with them. As they reached the last hymn, he left to go back to the café, where a racial brawl had broken out. In the affray he was stabbed by two white teenagers. He returned to the church steps and fell dying at the feet of the people still singing a Passion hymn. They tended for him as well as they could but were unable to save his life. He died in the ambulance on the way to the hospital.

It was many months later that a woman came to the church and introduced herself as the mother of the murdered man. She had come down from her home in Manchester to visit the place where her son had died, and to meet the people who had cared for him in his last moments. Then she said words that none of us who heard her will ever forget.

"I want you to know", she said, "that I have learned through this tragedy how great is God's love. There is no one a mother can love more than her son and no loss can be greater than to see him die. But that is what God suffered for us. He saw His Son die, but He never stopped loving us. We must allow such love to fill our hearts too, not to condemn, but to save those who sin against us."

Only the strength of such faith can break the stranglehold of old enmities and set us free for a new future. Therein lies the true Christian hope.

----------- * -----------

The People that walked in darkness have seen a great light.

The prophet was promising that a light would come into the world that no kind of darkness would ever be able to extinguish. On this First Advent Sunday we light a candle for the people who have shown that to be true – people who have come out of the gloom of slavery into the light of freedom; people who have endured the humiliation of racism and have not lost their dignity; people who have learned to wait patiently and work expectantly for the coming of the Kingdom; people who in the face of death itself have seen the rays of eternal life. This is the good news. The light shines on in the dark and no darkness can overcome it.

The Collect for the First Sunday in Advent

Almighty God,
give us grace to cast away the works of darkness
and to put on the armour of light,
now in the time of this mortal life,
in which Your Son Jesus Christ
    came to us in great humility:
so that on the last day,
when He shall come again in His glorious majesty
    to judge the living and the dead,
we may rise to the life immortal;
through Him Who is alive and reigns
    with You and the Holy Spirit,
one God, now and for ever.

Advent Two

And two is for the prophets,
And for the light they bring.
They are candles in the darkness,
All alight for Christ the King.

THE PROPHETS

In the great white and yellow marquee that had been
pitched on the grounds of the University of British
Columbia in Vancouver, people were gathering from
all parts of the world for a special service of worship.
It marked the beginning of the Sixth Assembly of the
World Council of Churches, with its theme "Jesus
Christ the Life of the World". The worshippers
streamed in through the tent's open bays, coming
from all directions, robed in a rainbow of colours,
some wearing symbols of ancient Christian traditions,
others clad in modern garb. It seemed as though the
Holy Church throughout all the world were assembled
there in that tent of meeting. In procession, through
the midst of them, were carried two candles, and the
Book they all shared – the Holy Bible, from where
they would hear read daily the words of the prophets
and the proclamation of the Gospel, the very Word of
life.

In the opening worship there was a second procession too, of people coming to the altar with

offerings representing gifts they had received from God to sustain their lives – bread and rice, wine and water, yam and pineapple, music and art, even sports gear and games. Finally, as focus of all, a new-born baby, a little girl, was brought by her mother, who had come from Zimbabwe, one of the youngest nations present among us.

As the presiding minister, Philip Potter, cradled the baby in his arms, memories stirred in the minds of many of those present, memories of a struggle for life which had engulfed Zimbabwe only a few years before. It was one in which Philip's own voice had been among the prophets, warning the world of the catastrophe that would overtake that land if its leaders continued to be deaf to the voice of the racially oppressed among them. The World Council of Churches, of which Philip was then General Secretary, had tried to respond to the cries of anguish from those locked in mortal combat in a battle for self-determination. Through its programme to combat racism, it had given humanitarian aid to people suffering in the struggle and had pleaded their cause before the conscience of the nations, urging them to work for the peace that comes not from victory on a battlefield but from the justice that makes reconciliation possible. At last, after years of warfare and months of tardy negotiation, the new nation had come into being. To many people gathered in that tent of meeting from nations still struggling for justice it must have seemed that life always is a fight against the forces of death. Birth comes only out of travail and pain.

When the new life is born, the travail is forgotten in the joy. As the new-born infant was presented at the altar, all rejoiced together that God had once more entrusted to human hands the care of one of His little ones. The world seemed again a place of hope.

It was in a place of worship that the great "prophet of the Advent" first heard the call of God. Isaiah was a city man, a faithful servant of his king, a proud and prosperous ruler. But the king had been brought low by sickness and none of his wealth could save him. Pondering on the frailty of life, feeling sorrowful in heart and dejected in spirit, Isaiah waits in the Temple to hear what God is saying through this apparently devastating circumstance. Everything seems to be falling apart now that the king has gone. Without strong leadership, the nation will be a ready prey for its enemies; the moral laxity of the people has weakened their military strength; even the Temple worship is becoming neglected. But it is there in the Temple that Isaiah sees where the true King reigns. He sees the Lord seated as it were on the throne of the universe, the whole of heaven and earth filled with His glory. Then he hears that same Lord, not giving a message, but calling for a messenger to speak to the people. Isaiah responds, probably surprising even himself, "Here am I; send me." Like every prophet before him, he is conscious of a sense of inadequacy and unworthiness. He feels himself stained with the sins of the society in which he lives. But he is assured of God's purging forgiveness. He is set free to prophesy.

It is not an easy message he is given to deliver, for it is one of condemnation on those who continue to disobey the word of God. Then gradually into the sense of doom breaks through a dawn of hope. All the subsequent prophecies of "Isaiah", and there is a threefold library of them, become filled with anticipation of the coming of a King who will not only rule the people of Israel justly, but will govern all the nations upon the earth and guide their feet into the way of peace. For us, many of the words of Isaiah have become so inextricably woven into the music of Handel's *Messiah*, and so associated with memories of Christmas past, that it is hard to hear them as the great good news for the future that they were when they were first announced. It was not that the prophets in the books of Isaiah were foretelling in detail any future events. The prophets did not forth-tell; they called forth the people to take fresh hope and to trust that, with God's help and with His chosen leaders, they could shape a new future for themselves, which would become a fulfilment of God's promises.

Each of the books of Isaiah (and between them they cover a period of about three hundred years of history) was addressing an urgent present situation caused by a series of devastating crises: the defeat of Israel at the hand of the Assyrians, the Exile in Babylon and the disillusionment of the subsequent home-coming to a devastated land. The people of Israel had seen their land laid low, their hopes dashed by their enemies and their cities breaking down into lawlessness. Many remedies had been tried – armed might and rebellion, alliances with stronger nations, stricter enforcement of the law, but all to no avail. They felt that instead of their promised freedom, they had come into one kind of bondage after another.

The first prophet Isaiah begged a new king, Ahaz, to trust the promises of God, to act patiently and not to fear his enemies. Then the prophet said a strange thing. He said that, as a sign of God's good faith and the people's trust in Him, a child would be born to a young woman and the child's name would mean "God is with us." Before that child was two years old the king's enemies would be defeated and a new day would dawn: "A virgin shall conceive and bear a son and shall call his name Immanuel" (Isaiah 7:14). That child would be a sign of hope.

The king did not dare to trust so frail a sign, and the disaster descended. In the midst of the bloodshed and the battle, the prophet still declared that it would be a royal child who would restore the people's fortune. The psalmist had proclaimed that when the nations raged against one another the only hope for peace would be that God would raise up a king in Israel whom all the kings on earth would be compelled to respect (Psalm 2). Now the prophet declares that the people must put their trust in the coming of such a king, anointed by God to rule wisely and well in a way that will lead all the nations into peace. Then Jerusalem will become once again a model city, a prototype for all the world of the very city of God:

For to us a child is born,
to us a Son is given;
and the government shall be upon His shoulder,
and His name will be called
Wonderful Counsellor, Mighty God, Everlasting
   Father,
Prince of Peace.

Isaiah 9:6; RSV

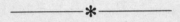

Harare, the capital of Zimbabwe, formerly known as Salisbury, must be one of the most elegant of modern cities. Its broad, tree-lined thoroughfares, its spacious parks, its bold architecture, remain in tribute to planners who thought they were building for a privileged society to last a thousand years, but whose skills have now endowed a multi-racial community with a metropolis of which they can all be proud. It was in the flower-decked Harare Gardens that we gathered to record "Songs of Praise" for a programme scheduled to be shown on BBC television on the Second Sunday in Advent. Choirs had come in bus loads from the black townships beyond the suburbs, and fleets of cars had brought people from the still predominantly white cathedral choir. There was a Salvation Army band, a young people's orchestra and a team of African drummers. Everyone had learned all the hymns, whether they were in English or in Shona or in Ndebele. Each hymn had its own conductor, coaxing that vast congregation to sing over and over again, standing, swaying, dancing, clapping, all in the blaze of an African afternoon sun, until the producers and their Zimbabwean camera crew were satisfied that sound and picture were the best they could be. There was an enormous sense of enjoyment of one another's music, and a genuine commitment to demonstrating that here in this land they were seeing at least part of the Advent prophecy coming true, as together in Christ they could acclaim the One who is the

> Dear desire of every nation,
> Joy of every loving heart.

For me, in the making of this particular programme, the most memorable moment was not in the singing of hymns but in the reading of the Scripture passage. Partly it was the impact of the passage's being read by the one who was at that time President of the nation, the Rev. Canaan Banana; partly it was the reverent sincerity with which he, himself a Methodist preacher, recited rather than read the words. But most impressive of all was his choice of the Scripture passage. It was from the prophet Isaiah, Chapter 2 verses 2 to 4:

> They shall beat their swords into ploughshares and
>   their spears into pruning hooks.
> Nation shall not lift up sword against nation, neither
>   shall they learn war any more.

The day before we recorded the hymns in the park, we had been at the Presidential Palace to talk with the President about his hopes for this nation now that independence had been achieved. Had the past left unhealed scars and was there still a sense of unavenged wrongs? The keynote of his answer was the one word: reconciliation.

"We have not rounded up our war criminals nor sought revenge against those who imprisoned us", he said. "We welcome all who will help us build a genuine peace in the new Zimbabwe."

Ironically, just as he spoke those words there was a burst of gunfire. It came from the barracks next door where the army was having rifle practice! Feeling that this was hardly a suitable background sound for a conversation about peace, the President gave orders for at least an hour's silence until the interview was over. It was a salutary reminder that even a country at peace within itself has a need for defence along its borders. Zimbabwe remains one of southern Africa's "front-line states". So it made all the more poignant the President's exposition of the prophetic passage. He saw it not as a prediction of a passive peace, but of an active war against the hunger and poverty which are still the great enemies of the people.

"We need desperately those ploughshares and pruning-hooks," he insisted, "so how tragic it is that we still have to go on purchasing guns."

Peace had become one of the great themes of all the prophets who make up the collected writings of the book of Isaiah. It was not merely the peace that was the absence of war that they anticipated. They looked rather for a peace that would come through the restoration of justice and a concern for the welfare of the whole community, the peace of *shalom*, a totally healthy society.

The first Isaiah, an urban gentleman, had been ashamed of the city in which he lived. He saw it as a diseased place where people had lost any sense of healthy values. He despised the women who minced about in their fancy shoes and expensive fashions. He loathed the merchant men who lived solely by monetary considerations. He hated the religious hypocrisy of those who thought they could buy themselves into God's favour. He wept over the injustices done to the poor in corrupt courts and by merciless money-lenders. He pleaded with his nation's leaders in direct and simple terms:

"Cease to do evil, learn to do good; seek justice and correct oppression; defend the fatherless, plead for the widow" Isaiah 1:17.

Yet he never gave up hope. He believed it was still possible for the people to make a fresh start. If only they would come back to God in penitence, He would have mercy upon them. All the blood of their guilt could be washed away and they could once again be people of clean hands and a pure heart. Then indeed would the city of Jerusalem be seen as a model for all cities, a place where people lived according to the precepts of God's law. For a city at peace within itself would draw the wondering eyes of all the nations, and peace would prevail throughout the world.

World peace is a theme that grows even stronger through the later books of Isaiah, particularly in the best known and most quoted passages of all, in the second Isaiah, chapters 40–45. These were addressed to a people in exile, and their emphasis became placed more and more strongly on the universality of God's reign. Not only does God have a plan for all the nations upon earth, but it is a cosmic plan too. This second Isaiah is a visionary who draws much of his inspiration from the starry heavens and the vastness of the ocean. He comes to see that there are no bounds to the power of God, the Creator of the whole universe.

This God holds all nations in His hands, even those whom Israel had regarded as their enemies. The prophet dares to suggest that the restoration of Israel will come about through the intervention of a Persian king, Cyrus, whom the Lord will use in the fulfilment of His purposes for all people. This must have been a most controversial claim to make – rather like suggesting in our day that one of God's unwitting agents in edging the world toward peace might be President Gorbachev! But the prophet suggests that God's ways are not our ways. They are not to be questioned, but only followed if they are leading the world into a time of reconstruction and reconciliation.

Like the first Isaiah, the second too is deeply immersed in the worshipping life of his community. He longs to see the Temple cleansed, and priest and people adorning themselves in greater purity of life and raiment. Through them the city of Jerusalem could be a place where instruction in God's law is given to the whole nation and indeed to the whole world. The effect of such purity of life would be felt not only by the people but even by the animal creation and the natural world. It would produce a new economy and a new ecology. Israel must see its mission as that of caretaker for the whole of creation. When the people have once again learned obedience to the law, then the crops will flourish, and the trees will grow and the whole community will live joyously in the light of God's promises:

> For you shall go out with joy and be led forth in
>   peace.
> The mountains and hills before you
> shall break forth into singing
> and all the trees of the field shall clap their hands.
>
> Isaiah 55:12-13; RSV

In our short stay in Zimbabwe there was one young lady I was eager to meet — Mvuselelo Nyoni, that Vancouver baby, who by this time was four years old and to be found playing happily among her friends in a nursery school in Bulawayo. She was just old enough to enjoy looking at the photographs that recalled her ecumenical début. Her mother's commitment to all that the ecumenical movement stands for has intensified with the years, and she has dedicated her life to working among the rural women of Zimbabwe. Their problems are daunting. As in many a nation, the needs of rural people, especially those of the women who do most of the agricultural work, are not high on the country's development plans. These women often have a long trek to find fresh water and carry it back to their families; the work in the fields is back-breaking when they have little in the way of mechanized equipment; the learning of new skills is a slow process to those who have had small chance to become literate. But they are encouraged to develop whatever resources they have within themselves, to determine their own needs, to use their own strength. So we saw them breaking up rocks to make a road through a waste place; building dams to conserve their water supplies; planting crops in rotation to ensure a better harvest; co-operating to gather and market their produce.

It is hard work, but the women respond well and enjoy taking responsibility for improving the condition of their own lives and that of their children. Their sense of community is strong, and they take pride in being able to give as well as to receive aid. When we went into one of the villages to film for our television programme, they had decided to take a day off work in the fields and to sing for us one of their own Advent lyrics, accompanied by drums and dancing. They watched the lengthy preparations the camera team had to make, intrigued by the apparatus and puzzled as to why it took so long to set it all up. It amused them when they were asked again and again to repeat their performance. Sometimes it was because a cloud had passed over the sun, temporarily changing the lighting effect; once a cow walked right across the shot; on another take, chickens squawked at the wrong moment. Even when at last it seemed that all had gone well the sound engineer reported odd noises coming through his headphones. It took some time to detect the source – a baby snoozing peacefully on its mother's back. But at last the producer was satisfied, the baby could sleep on and the women were invited to rest after their energetic dancing in what was by now the noon-time sun.

Instead they took us all by surprise. Those who only a few minutes before had been flagging in energy and sweating in the sun suddenly began dancing again, not stamping their feet rhythmically as before, but actually going down on their knees, and moving forward in formation towards the production team. In their hands now they were carrying gifts – a basket, a bowl, a bouquet of flowers, and, for the cameramen, five dollars to buy a drink. The men were reluctant to accept the money, far too great a sum for so poor a community to give. But the women insisted. It was their privilege and their joy to provide for the needs of their visitors. Nor was that all. For some time, even during the dancing, we had heard excited noises coming from one of the huts. There was the rattling of pans, the clinking of cutlery and the chatter of voices. It sounded like the frenzied activity of a church catering committee going about their business preparing a sit-down meal. And that was exactly what it was. Luncheon had been prepared for us. "Come," they said, "all is now ready", and we sat down to a sumptuous feast prepared for us as honoured guests by those to whom food and drink were the most precious things they had to give.

"Come, for all is now ready", said the servant in the parable Jesus told of the banquet that would be held in the Kingdom of God (Luke 14:17). But though the meal was ready, the guests were not. They all had worthy excuses, based on the values of a virtuous society – a business transaction, a farming responsibility, a family obligation. No conscientious person could be expected to give a party priority over such important engagements, unless, that is, the host were someone of even greater importance. An invitation bearing a royal crest and a palace address might well have persuaded them to rearrange their schedule. Most of us like to be seen in the right kind of company.

It was clearly a royal banquet Jesus had in mind when He told this story, for it has many echoes of the prophet's words in Isaiah 25. There the prophet had envisaged a day when all the peoples of the world would sit down together at a "feast of fat things full of marrow, of wine on the lees well refined". It is hardly a menu to be recommended by a nutritionist, but it suggests the abundant hospitality of a generous host. The same symbolism is used in a recent award-winning Danish film, called *Babette's Feast*. It tells, in beautiful simplicity, the story of a pious and straitlaced community living in a remote village on the coast of Jutland. They have befriended a French refugee who for many years works among them as a serving maid. But on one glorious day she treats them to a magnificent banquet such as they have never seen before. It transpires that she was once the chef in one of the finest restaurants in Paris. The meal has a magic effect, relaxing rigid attitudes, breaking down social barriers, healing old quarrels. It is no wonder that a banquet has become the sign of the Messianic age.

In both prophecy and parable the emphasis is on the fact that no one is to be excluded from this banquet – neither the poor nor the prosperous, neither the Jew nor the Gentile. All sit down together in the Kingdom of God. The prophet adds a strange detail to his vision. It is as though there is still a veil over the mountain where the banquet has been prepared. The picture conjured up is rather like that scene in *Great Expectations* where the wedding feast lies rotting on the table of Miss Haversham's room, covered in cobwebs and dust, the meal abandoned because the love has died. There are still tears to be shed for our lost love of one another and our lost love of God. Yet the prophet foresees the time when the grief will be comforted. God will wipe away all tears from our eyes. Hudson Taylor, the great missionary to China, once commented on this promise saying, "I would not wish then to be one of those who had no tears to wipe away".

It is those who have known real hunger who most appreciate the food offered by the generous host and it is those who have shed genuine tears who are led to the springs of a joy sparkling with hope. Like the prophet, they look forward to the day when it will be said,

"Lo, this is our God, we have waited for Him, that He might save us. This is the Lord; we have waited for Him; let us be glad and rejoice in His salvation!"   Isaiah 25:9.

Father Philemon is a jovial man. When he smiles, the grin spreads right across his round, black face, and when he talks it is with an open and an optimistic faith, undaunted by the dire things that went on not so long ago in the parish near Harare where he now ministers. Once the township was a headquarters of guerrilla activity. Some of the church members had themselves given up hope of achieving their freedom without taking up arms. The whole district was suspected of supporting the rebel fighters and so was kept under surveillance and constantly raided. People were intimidated both by government forces and by guerrilla bands. In the midst of so much hostility and fear, the church went on trying to carry out its ministry to those fighting for their freedom, those defending their land and those caught in the crossfire.

Philemon himself was then a young man, sickened by all that he saw of the endless spiral of violence and the indiscriminate suffering it caused. He resolved that the rest of his life would be spent in a ministry of reconciliation. So he offered for the priesthood in the

Anglican Church. I did not need to ask if he is happy in his work. His whole being radiates joy and enthusiasm. He sums up his message in one simple word: Love.

"It's love we need most", he said, "to drive out the fear, to build up the trust and to set people truly free for one another and for God".

In his ministry of both Word and Sacrament, that love finds expression from the pulpit and in the playground, at the communion table and in the community hall. His ministry of reconciliation means bringing people together across the still wide racial gap, in both worship and recreation. The pot of tea shared in a multi-racial fellowship meeting may seem a small enough gesture but it can be a foretaste of the Kingdom of God. The game enjoyed together on a sports field can help to dispel old, grotesque stereotypes and to restore normal human relationships.

"They need to know that we don't have horns, even if we don't have haloes either", he joked.

I could almost guess what he would choose as his favourite hymn for our Advent Songs of Praise

> This is the day that the Lord has made
> We will rejoice and be glad in it.

Both priest and prophet, Philemon looks forward confidently to the coming day of the Lord.

"Today", said Jesus, "this Scripture has been fulfilled in your ears" (Luke 4:21). What a striking opening sentence for a sermon! No wonder the congregation sat up to listen attentively. Here was the local carpenter's son quoting one of their favourite passages from the prophets (Isaiah 61:1-2). The hope the third Isaiah had given to the exiles returning to Jerusalem was being given to the Jews living under Roman rule. Now there was good news, Jesus was claiming, for the poor; there would be liberty for the oppressed; the acceptable year of the Lord had arrived. The people nodded to one another approvingly. God had raised up another prophet among them.

Scholars are not sure whether Jesus deliberately chose this passage or whether it was the one appointed in an assigned lectionary. Neither is it known for certain whether it would have been read in Hebrew or in Jesus' own language, Aramaic. It is notable, however, that there are some slight differences between the prophet's words and Jesus' rendering of them. Jesus omits two phrases of the original – "to heal the broken-hearted" and a reference to "a day of vengeance of our God". It seems as though His version deliberately suppressed the negative aspects of Isaiah's message and stressed the positive ones.

As a preacher Jesus followed the rabbinic tradition of illustrating the texts of one prophet by references to others. He quotes both Elijah and Elisha as evidence of His theme that God's love is not confined only to the people of Israel, but reaches out through them to the people of all nations. So He tells the story of the hungry widow of Sidon, a Phoenician town, who was helped by Elijah; and of the Syrian captain, Naaman, who was healed by Elisha, stressing the compassionate humanity of men who in his hearers' minds would be associated with a stern, religious zeal for the defence of Israel and Israel's God.

His words enrage His congregation so much that we shall never know how the sermon would have ended. He is hurled from the synagogue. But He remains confident of His vocation. No longer can He remain the carpenter of Nazareth. Now His mission is to travel throughout Judea, preaching the good news to the poor, healing the sick, opening the eyes of the blind, proclaiming in both word and deed the coming of that Kingdom which the prophets had foretold.

It was in Bulawayo, the country town whose architecture recalls its colonial past, that we met two old men who in prophetic ways had done much between them to shape Zimbabwe's history. Appropriately we interviewed them in a school, for education had been the priority of both their lives. They had met over fifty years before, the one a missionary from New Zealand, the other a local schoolboy. They were both destined for important spells of leadership – the former as Prime Minister of the country, the latter as Headmaster of a school.

Garfield Todd came to Southern Rhodesia, as it was then known, in the 1930s, to preach the Gospel. The mandate of his Lord seemed clear enough to him:

"Go and make disciples of all nations, baptizing them everywhere in the name of the Father and the Son and the Holy Spirit, teaching them to observe all that I have commanded you. And lo, I am with you always to the close of the age".

He soon discovered that such a mission involved him in manifold activities. Preaching the Gospel to the poor among whom he worked meant caring enough for them to pull out the aching tooth, to attend the birth of a child, to help repair a leaking roof, to take a grievance to the District Commissioner, to proclaim in every way, in word and deed, the all-embracing love of God. So he found himself acting as dentist, doctor, plumber, social worker, school master and preacher. He longed to see the people achieving all the potential that was in them, learning to read the Bible for themselves, training for leadership on the land and in the community.

For Garfield himself, his commitment to a Gospel that touched every part of people's lives took him inevitably along the road that leads from prayer to politics. Eventually, in a colony which had a measure of self-government, he achieved the highest office, raising his voice within the courts of Parliament on behalf of those who were still voiceless there, but whose needs were clamant in his ears. Few of those who had power to change things were prepared to listen to him, and he was not long in office. Later, in the years of Rhodesia's unilateral independence, he was for a brief time in prison instead. But his zeal for Zimbabwe has never flagged, and in the new nation he has an honoured and respected place.

I asked him in the television interview what gift he would most like to bequeath to the land that has become his by adoption. He grinned broadly, and placed his hand on the arm of David – his African companion and first pupil.

"The people we love", he replied, "those whom we have been privileged to teach and who are now themselves responsible for the training of a new generation of citizens – this is our best legacy to Zimbabwe."

I asked David what his best gift to Zimbabwe would be.

"Faith", he answered directly, "people who have faith in themselves, in their country and in God."

How did he hope to pass such faith on to young people growing up in a different world from the one he had known? With a touching simplicity he replied.

"We tell them the old, old story, the same story we heard. You will hear the children singing it for you today:

Yes, Jesus loves me
The Bible tells me so."

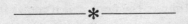

To St Paul, the Hebrew Bible was one of the sources of his authority. He reminds the Christians in Rome (Romans 15:4) that the words of the prophets are meant for all of us, Jews and Gentiles, to encourage us and to teach us patience with one another as we wait together for the full revealing of God's purposes. Paul sees the Scriptures as a unifying factor in the life of the early Church. He recalls from many parts of the Scriptures – the psalms, the Pentateuch, the prophets – verses which call on the Gentiles to join in the praises of God. He reminds the Christians in Rome that the covenant made with Abraham was one that extended through him to all the peoples of the earth. He traces how Jesus, Himself firmly rooted in a Jewish lineage, came first to be the servant of the Jews and then to embrace within the compass of His love the whole of humanity.

"Welcome one another therefore," writes St Paul, "as Christ has welcomed you." There had been difficulties in that Christian congregation in Rome over the different dietary customs of Jews and Gentiles; there had been arguments about which festivals to observe; there had been disputes over the interpretation of texts. All of these Paul begs the people to lay aside. He urges them to model their behaviour towards one another on Christ's acceptance of them all. They must learn to respect each other's traditions, passing no judgements, loving one another unconditionally and living together in the one hope they can all share, the hope which comes from faith in God.

———————— * ————————

It was a long climb up to the mission village where we were to light our second Advent candle. Our journey had taken us from the centre of things in Harare out to the Eastern Highlands of Zimbabwe, on to the border with Mozambique. There we were to meet a tiny congregation in a hamlet belonging to a Catholic mission, far too remote to send people to the Harare Gardens to join the other congregations for our Songs of Praise.

Our journey out to the mission in our hired cars had been hazardous. Apart from the mechanical breakdowns, a failed clutch and later a flat tyre, we had rough roads to negotiate, with frequent stops to photograph the weird and fascinating rock formations and on occasion the irresistible wild life. It was impossible to do the whole journey by car. Eventually we had to park at the central mission compound on the hillside, and do the rest of the journey on foot. We scrambled down into a swampy valley and up steep slopes again until we could see the little group of thatched huts in the distance. Despite the lateness of our arrival, which had kept the people waiting several hours, our welcome was deafening. Even as we appeared over the horizon, the women began what I can only describe as a joyous hullabaloo, though it is an inadequate word to capture the strange ululating cry with which they always express their welcome.

In the hut that served as their place of meeting, they had prepared a table for us. It was the only piece of furniture in the room except for a wooden cupboard full of pots and pans. The earth floor had been swept, and cloths had been put down for us to sit on.

Quickly, all the children crowded in, scrambling to be
near the front so as to see what was going on. The
adults gathered more sedately, and a little shyly as the
Advent wreath was reverently brought in and placed
on the table. The lighting technician struggled hard in
the darkness of the windowless hut to provide enough
illumination to make filming possible. Then the
singing started – words painstakingly learned by rote
in a language few people beyond the schoolmaster and
some of his pupils understood. They were words
describing an experience remote in history and culture
from their own, and yet echoing a yearning for
freedom that they could well identify with. It was a
hymn we had chosen to be sung in all the places where
we were lighting the Advent candles:

> O come, O come Immanuel,
> And ransom captive Israel –
> Rejoice, rejoice, Immanuel
> Shall come to thee, O Israel.

As Maria, a lovely lithe African teenager, came
forward to light the candle I thought of how in that
moment those faithful followers of Christ were linked
with the privileged students of Trinity College,
Cambridge, where our Advent journey had begun,
and the children of the city streets of Edinburgh where
the third candle would be lit, and the vast congregation on the other side of the world in Vancouver,
where our Advent waiting would end. Maybe it was
that extraordinary sense of the ties linking the
faithful across the world, or maybe it was the
powerful gleam of that one candle in the cavernous

darkness, but somehow I have never felt so aware of the message of Advent as I did in that small village on the hillside of Zimbabwe. The ululations sounded then like Hallelujahs welcoming the coming King.

"How beautiful are the feet of them that preach us the gospel of peace."

The People's Creed

I believe in a colour-blind God,
Maker of technicolour people,
Who created the universe and provided abundant
    resources,
For equitable distribution among all His people.

I believe in Jesus Christ,
Born of a common woman,
Who was ridiculed, disfigured and executed,
Who on the third day rose and fought back;
He storms the highest councils of men,
Where He overturns the iron rule of injustice.
From henceforth He shall continue
To judge the hatred and arrogance of men.

I believe in the Spirit of reconciliation,
The united body of the dispossessed;
The communion of the suffering masses,

The power that overcomes the dehumanizing forces
  of men;
The resurrection of personhood, justice and
  equality,
And in the final triumph of Brotherhood.

Canaan Banana
From *The Gospel according to the Ghetto*

We light this second Advent candle to commemorate
all prophets who have proclaimed the coming of the
Kingdom of God and have worked for His reign of
justice and peace; and we pray that God may bless
Africa, guide her rulers and grant her peace.

Collect for the Second Sunday in Advent

Blessed Lord,
Who caused all holy scriptures to be written for our
  learning:
help us so to hear them,
to read, mark, learn and inwardly digest them
that, through patience, and the comfort of Your
  holy word,
we may embrace and for ever hold fast the hope of
  everlasting life,
which You have given us in our Saviour, Jesus
  Christ.

Advent Three

And three for John the Baptist.
He calls on us to sing:
"O prepare the way for Jesus Christ,
He is coming, Christ the King."

JOHN THE BAPTIST

I first saw the musical *Godspell* in a small theatre off Broadway in New York, while it was still relatively unknown. It had been described to me as a musical comedy based on the Gospel of Matthew, produced as part of a students' exercise in modern composition. I took my seat in the stalls somewhat sceptically, expecting to be deafened by the din and dissatisfied with the content.

Then there fell a hush of anticipation as the lights dimmed in the theatre, and the solitary note of a horn penetrated the silence. A shadowy figure came down the aisle of the auditorium, and for the first time I heard that haunting opening solo, "Prepare ye the way of the Lord". I knew then that this was no student romp. This was heralding a reverent presentation of a story that would kindle our imagination in new ways, and yet remain faithful to the old text, particularly in the prelude to the ministry of Jesus, the preaching of John the Baptist.

Then abruptly the mood changed. From the solemn

note of warning the music became a dance of joy. Joy seems a strange word to associate with John the Baptist, a man of austere and ascetic practice. Yet this Third Sunday in Advent, when we light the candle especially for him, is known also as Laetare Sunday, the Sunday to rejoice. "Rejoice in the Lord always", writes St Paul, "Again I say Rejoice."

The joy of John the Baptist was evident even before he was born. His mother felt him leap for joy within her womb when she first heard her cousin Mary announce that she was expecting the birth of Jesus. When John is a grown man and hears of the beginning of Jesus' ministry, he compares himself to the best man at a wedding, rejoicing for and with the bridegroom as they await the arrival of the bride. "This joy, this perfect joy is now mine", he says (John 3:29). "As he grows greater, I must grow less." The joy of John the Baptist is the joy of a humble man, confident of where his own vocation begins and ends.

It was in Central America that I met a modern Baptist, not as rugged as John, but with that same quiet spring of joy, welling up from a deep spirituality refreshing many who are at present enduring a wilderness experience. Gustavo Parajon is the leader of the Baptist community in Nicaragua. The hand of destiny has seemed to be upon him since childhood. His devout parents committed him to the Lord as soon as he was born, and brought him up to take a pride in his Protestant heritage. In those days that demanded a lot of a little boy in Latin America. In the State school he attended the religious instruction was Roman Catholic, and, although he was permitted to be withdrawn from the lessons, he did not escape taunting from the other children, and even on occasion stoning, for being of a different faith. But he stood his ground firmly, refusing to fight back. When he grew older he made his own confession of faith, was baptized and became a minister of the Gospel, following in the way his parents had pointed him.

Today times have changed radically in Nicaragua. In a land where there are now some two thousand evangelical pastors, and about a fifth of the population are Protestants, the ecumenical climate is a much warmer one. The freedom of religion enjoyed by all faiths makes it possible for the Parajons to send their own children to a Roman Catholic school with no fear of discrimination or of pressure to conform to the Catholic Church, which still has a powerful influence in the country. Dr Parajon himself is a highly respected member of the whole community. At the time of the earthquake in 1972 it was he who called the people of many different denominations together to provide food and clothing for the victims, whatever their faith. From that small beginning grew a new form of ministry. The Protestant Relief Agency, CEPAD, is one of the major bodies in the country working to relieve the distress of those who, through war or natural disaster, have seen their homes destroyed and their crops devastated. Dr Parajon himself has never lost sight of the vision that inspired it all – the call to prepare the way for the coming of good news for the poor, healing for the sick and peace for those of good will.

This involves not only relief work but also positive reconstruction, as the people are encouraged to work co-operatively on the land, to share in the widespread literacy campaigns, to help build roads across the mountains and erect clinics in the distant villages. *"The Gospel of Peace"*, proclaims a poster on the walls of the CEPAD office, *"is a struggle for life." "This is our land, this is our liberation!"*

The songs of liberation resound across the mountains of Nicaragua. Wherever people gather for worship, whatever their theology might be, hope beats in their hymns and joy strums out on their guitars. It springs not only from a natural, Latin American exuberance but from a sense of expectancy, of confidence in the future. In one small Baptist church we visited, we were astounded when the service began with what we thought was the British national anthem. Only when the Spanish words were translated for us did we realize that this was a hymn hailing the coming of the King of Heaven. In what we were told was a traditional Mass, celebrated by Cardinal Obando Bravo in the presence of a great crowd of worshippers, the singing was charismatic in quality, with nuns and priests clapping their hands and uplifting their arms like delighted children waiting to receive the gifts of a loving Father. In the Peasants' Church, which has its own setting of a Campesino Mass, we were soon caught up in the rhythms of the Gloria:

With the most joyful sound of my people
I come to sing
this glory to Christ.
I want to sing to Jesus
who is the leader of truth.
who has the overflowing and explosive
glee of the fireworks
that illumine our skies
at the popular fiesta.
Glory to the one who follows the Gospel,
who denounces injustice without fear.
Glory to the one who suffers prison and exile
and gives his life fighting the oppressor.

As we sang, I looked up and saw in a vivid, vibrant mural beside me the portrait of one of Central America's modern martyrs, Archbishop Oscar Romero, a man, who, like John the Baptist, at the cost of his own life, had made way for his Lord and followed the Gospel.

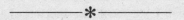

The portrait of John the Baptist in the four gospels is one of the most compelling in the whole biblical pageant. He is the only person whose appearance, dress and even diet are described to us in detail, as he emerges from the desert, a living link with the prophets of old. A mysterious but in no way legendary figure, he is definitively placed by St Luke in a historical setting. His ministry begins in the fifteenth year of the Emperor Tiberius (i.e. AD 28–29) and during the High Priesthood of Annas and Caiaphas. His location "in the wilderness" is not so exact, but it may have been Qumran, where some of the faithful remnant had taken refuge as they awaited the coming of the Messiah. He emerges from that wilderness like some wild man, with a voice "like the roar of a lion in the desert", as Jerome puts it. He has a message which echoes that of Isaiah himself. Matthew, Mark and Luke all quote the same text as testimony to this continuity, though it takes a little juggling with the original Hebrew, or at least with the punctuation, to make it fit exactly:

> "The voice of one crying: 'In the wilderness prepare ye the way of the Lord'" (Isaiah 40:3)

becomes in the gospels

> "The voice of one crying in the wilderness: 'Prepare ye the way of the Lord'" (Mark 1:3)

The annunciation of John's conception and the story of his birth have overtones of the advent of patriarchs and prophets. Like Sara, the mother of Isaac, John's mother Elizabeth rejoices in pregnancy that comes late in her life, a special sign of the Lord's favour. Like Elkanah, the father of Samuel, Zechariah waits for exact instructions from God to know what his son shall be called and how he is to be dedicated to the Lord's service. He is given a prophetic rather than a family name – John, meaning "Yahweh is gracious". The hymn celebrating his birth, the Benedictus, has rung down the centuries in the liturgy of the Church alongside that of the Magnificat itself.

It is no wonder that this stern figure should have attracted the attention of artists down the ages. One of the early ikons gives him the wings of an angel befitting his "angelic", heraldic role, a rough body almost like a wolf's and eyes as penetrating as a tiger's. The fifteenth century artist, Lucas Cranach, depicts him as a popular preacher using a tree trunk as his pulpit and attracting a motley crowd of young and old, rich and poor. Rodin's statue portrays an agile, taut figure, his hand poised in rhetorical gesture, for whom, the story goes, the model was a poor but passionate peasant who came to the artist's studio demanding work. In a massive stone sculpture in St Juan, the Puerto Rican artist Rafael Lopez del Campo plants St John the Baptist firmly on solid feet, grounded on rock, his index finger pointing insistently to the heavens, one of the "signs of contradiction" so much needed in our modern world.

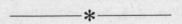

The road out from Managua taking us towards the mountains was at first pleasantly rural. The peaceful scene was disturbed only by the scuffling of cattle being driven out of the way of our mini-bus by cowboys, their panama hats cocked on the back of their heads, as with cheeky grins they waved us on our journey. Soon the country opened out into more bush-like scenery, reminiscent of the African veld. Then we arrived at a town, which we were told was the beginning of the military zone, where the road had only a few days before been blown up by mines laid by the Contras, the forces opposing the Sandanista Government. From there on, the way became more steep and we were conscious of a stronger military presence.

We eventually reached the town of Matagalpa, a straggling community built up a slope, rather like an Italian hillside village. Women in aprons were standing in the doorways gossiping or going off to market. We went there too and wandered alongside the trays set out on the ground, laden with fruit and fresh vegetables. We ducked under the racks of clothes above our heads, most of them obviously second-hand. We paused at the many stalls selling leather craft and basket work, intended for the now almost non-existent tourist trade. We bought our souvenirs and some lunch, and set off on the next stage of our journey along country lanes threading through dark wooded hills. It was easy, though nerve-wracking, to imagine sudden ambushes by hostile forces. But we proceeded safely on our way, and as we journeyed our companion Pedro told us his story.

He had grown up in one of those mountain villages, where even then there had been fierce fighting between the peasant followers of the rebel leader Sandino and the wealthy landowners who virtually ruled the country and exploited the people. His father had fought and been killed in the service of Sandino. His mother had been left to live solely on her weaving, eking out a living for herself and her children as best she could. As soon as he was old enough, Pedro had gone off to a plantation to pick coffee. He was a well-behaved, intelligent boy and he worked hard, and so attracted the attention of the plantation owner who offered to adopt him and give him a much better chance in life.

At first, the lure of riches tempted him. They would give him the chance he longed for – to go to college and to embark on a successful career, as a lawyer perhaps or a schoolteacher. But the memory of his father's sacrifice for the sake of the poor haunted him, and he felt it would be a betrayal if he so easily, as it were, changed sides. So he left the plantation and went back to his own people, identifying with them in their struggle for justice. Under the draconian rule of Samoza, he was captured, imprisoned and kept in solitary confinement. The only book he was allowed to read was the Bible. But it was that book that opened his eyes. It seemed to be endorsing the very struggle to which he had committed his life. It told of the centuries through which the prophets of God had pronounced judgement on the rich and proclaimed God's bias for the poor. It held out promise for the future of one who would come from God to set the people free and to fulfil His promise made to previous generations:

"That we, being delivered from the hand of our enemies might serve Him without fear in holiness and righteousness before Him all the days of our life."

Luke 1:73

He vowed then and there that he would commit the rest of his life to the service of this God and of His people.

The victory of the Sandinistas won for Pedro his release from prison. The programme they announced as their policy seemed to him to be one he could support in his new-found Christian commitment. Their priorities seemed to be the same as his. They promised to share power with the powerless, and to affirm the dignity of the poorest people. Pedro continued to work in the villages, serving now the co-operatives that grew up on land redistributed among the peasants. He helped the young widows of men fallen in battle to make a better livelihood than his mother had secured.

He took us to see some of them at work in his home town of Jinotega. We visited a hut where some twenty sewing machines, a consignment received from churches in California, were clattering away, as the women chattered even more loudly above the noise, turning out children's play clothes, selling at the equivalent of 75p a suit. Not far away, in a hillside co-operative, lived seventeen families, ninety people in all, in a cluster of houses among their small fields of beet, potatoes and beans. They had tried to build a school, but the building materials had run out. They were short of water, but there was no irrigation supply nearby. They would have liked to extend further into the mountains, but that was where the fighting was. The peasant leader, Miguel, a cheerful man with a toothless grin, took a philosophical view of it all.

"The Bible says there will always be wars," he said, "so we just have to get on and live our lives as best we can, and pray for a miracle."

"But you have to work for a miracle too", said Pedro.

"And that's mighty hard work", retorted Miguel cheerily.

Miguel invited me to visit his home, the wooden house he had built for his wife and six children. I counted only five clambering around their mother in the larger of the two rooms, and asked where the baby was. She took me into the bedroom. "Aqui", she said, pointing up. In the hammock swinging from the rafters a tiny child lay sleeping peacefully, unaware of the struggle it was still costing to enable her to survive and grow up into a saner world.

The full cost only became apparent to us when Pedro took us to the last place of call on this journey. He wanted to visit some of the young soldiers in the military hospital. It was one of the best tended places we had seen anywhere in Nicaragua. These victims of the fight to defend the revolution were certainly taken good care of. But the tragedy of so many broken bodies was an unbearable sight, and I noticed Pedro in tears as he stood beside the bed of a young seventeen-year-old whose legs had been blown off in the recent ambush by the Contras. It was the boy himself who spoke the words of hope.

"I still have my hands and my head with which to serve my people", he said.

We left in silence, anger welling up within us at the waste of life and the wanton destruction. How long, O

Lord, before the world heeds the warnings of the prophets and repents of its warfare?

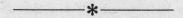

"Repentance", once said C. S. Lewis, "is no fun at all." In John the Baptist's book repentance was a rigorous word, no abstract term, but one that called for concrete acts of contrition and radical changes in behaviour. He was no preacher of honeyed words, but he was a master of invective. The magnetism that drew the crowds to him had a repulsive rather than an attractive force.

"You brood of vipers", he hissed at them. "Who warned you to flee from the wrath to come?"

People were compelled to stop and listen to this unorthodox oratory, even though he struck at the very roots of their confidence, their pride in their ancestry. They might regard themselves as children of Abraham, he stormed, but that meant nothing if they lived lives unworthy of their heritage.

When hearts were smitten with remorse, John responded not with moral platitudes but with frank, practical advice about what the people must do to amend their lives. Those in public service should stop taking bribes. Those in the army or police should stop harassing the people, and demanding higher wages for doing it. Those who were affluent should be more just and generous in their provision for the poor. It was as though John saw his role as that of sweeping the muck out of all the gutters of society, rather like the road cleaner who precedes a royal procession to make the way fit for a monarch to pass along.

Yet John himself was no respecter of persons. Even the monarch came in for the lashing of his tongue. He openly rebuked Herod the king for his lax moral behaviour in living with his sister-in-law, and as a result provoked royal wrath which finally wreaked its revenge. It was at the request of Herodias that John was imprisoned and eventually beheaded. But his reputation lived on, his voice still rang in people's ears, so much so that the King was even haunted by him, and feared that in Jesus John had come back from the dead to haunt him.

Despite all that John did to point beyond himself to the one whose way he had come to prepare, even twenty-five years after his death there were still to be found bands of his disciples, rehearsing all that he had taught them from the Scriptures, clinging to the hope they had found in the cleansing waters of his baptism, and patiently waiting for the coming of the promised one. He had prepared them well. When the leaders of the early Christian community in Ephesus, Priscilla and Aquila, met one of John's disciples, Apollos, they found a heart ready to receive the Gospel message and to spread it with the eloquence he had learned from the faithful prophet (Acts 18:24-28).

The greatest legacy of this lion of a man was the phrase he was the first to use in describing Jesus and what He had come to do. "Behold", he said, "the Lamb of God, who takes away the sin of the world." The prophet's roaring call to repentance had become the priest's promise of a sacrifice through which all may find their salvation.

The long queue of people lining up outside the Cathedral in Guatemala City were waiting, not for food to relieve their poverty but for the mercy of God, to have pity on them. Slowly the waiting thousands edged through the aisle of the great church to take their turn in standing before the massive crucifix and kissing the feet of the One before Whom, like them, John the Baptist had bowed in humility.

"O, Lamb of God, that takest away the sin of the world, have mercy – ten piedad, ten piedad", they murmured incessantly. For millions in Latin America, the crucifix has become the symbol of the solidarity of God with the suffering of humanity.

. In Guatemala it is a silent suffering. People were reluctant to speak to us about the atrocities of recent years and the terror that still haunts them, even in what seems to be a respite from the oppressive regimes of past dictators. Death squads still stalk the streets, the military presence is obvious and ubiquitous, the hands of big business operate the levers of power. The democratic government has promised to do what it can to combat the greatest enemy of the people, poverty, but, burdened by a national debt, it faces enormous economic problems. The largest areas of fertile land in the south are owned by a few wealthy families and are farmed to provide cash crops of bananas, coffee and cotton. The small-holdings of the peasant farmers are rarely more than two-acre plots, not large enough to yield sufficient food for a family. Most of the Indians own no land at all and have no means of subsistence. So many migrate to the city in the hope of finding work, but half the potential work force is unemployed. The political violence of the last decade has left in its wake some 120,000 orphan children, and though legally every child is entitled to primary education there are only enough schools to cater for half the population.

In their distress, the people turn to the Church for comfort and fortitude. Within the cathedral rich and poor mingle, powerful and powerless pray together, the Mass is celebrated for the overfed and the underpaid alike. But in the back streets of the slums the small "base communities", as they have come to be known, gather on their own to study their Bibles in search of words of hope.

We were invited to join one such Bible group at their Saturday night meeting. It was a clandestine occasion. There was a pre-arranged meeting in a café with a couple who took us on a bus out to the edge of the city, but we were warned to be discreet in our talking with them. At the end of the journey we were met by a guide who led us by the light of a torch through the side streets to the house of the group leader, the "animator" of the study. He took us along a dark alley to a shanty shed where the group itself had gathered – some twenty people, old and young together, perched on the two camp beds and five wooden chairs that filled the room. They welcomed us warmly, made room for us in the crowded space and invited us to join them in a song I recognized as coming from the Nicaraguan Peasant Mass:

You are the God of the poor,
the human and simple God,
the God who sweats in the street,
the God with the tanned face.

The passage appointed for study that evening was a difficult one – 2 Thessalonians Chapter 3. It seemed ironic to me that people who wanted work more than anything else were reading Paul's warning, "If anyone will not work, let him not eat". But then I learned a lesson. I discovered how different the Scriptures sound to those who hear in them an echo of their own experience. These people recognized in what St Paul was saying an affirmation of their own longing for the dignity of being able to earn their own living, and a strong condemnation of those who prosper in idleness, living off the sweat of other people's labours. In prayer they poured out before God their yearning for work, particularly for young people whose lives were in danger of rotting away through enforced idleness. Then they joined hands with us as we all prayed together, "Our Father – give us this day our daily bread – forgive us our trespasses" – and I have never been able to pray that prayer since without remembering that the "us" means all of us, including those people in Guatemala and many more hungry millions for whom this prayer is an urgent daily cry for mercy and for the very means of survival.

After the meeting, the animator took us back to his own home, a more spacious abode which he had built himself and which was adorned with a Christmas tree and one of the largest crib sets I have ever seen. It was crowded with miniature animals of all species and people of all nations, figures collected over many years. We were told that each year more dolls are added as a reminder of people the family has met or heard about, or wants to include in their prayers as the circle of their Christian love grows wider. So now, we shall be represented there in a tiny doll from Britain, a reminder that there is a place where we all meet, around the crib of the Lamb who came to take away the sin of the world.

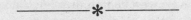

Just as John the Baptist required of the people concrete evidence of their repentance, so he required of Jesus actual proofs of His divine mission. Cut off from his cousin by his own gaol sentence, this courageous prophet seems to have been assailed by doubts as to whether the Kingdom of God really was at hand. Living as the prisoner of an earthly king must have made it difficult to believe in the rule of one who had come to set the captive free. Jesus sends His reply in words which John would well understand – no theological arguments, but vital accounts of events which are the authentic signs of the Kingdom: "The blind receive their sight and the lame walk, lepers are cleansed and the deaf hear, the dead are raised up and the poor have good news preached to them" (Luke 7:22).

The liberation brought by the Gospel is no mere formula for the future but a living experience of healing, of resurrection, of salvation here and now.

As He sends the message to John, Jesus recalls the character of this man who had caused such a sensation in his first appearing from the wilderness. In many ways the cousins could not have been more different from one another. John had few "comfortable words" to speak; he had no seamless robe to wear; he was no party-goer or pleasant companion on a country road. He seemed to want to take the Kingdom by storm rather than by patient steps, carrying a cross. But Jesus recognized in him the courage of a true prophet and paid him the greatest compliment he paid to any man:

"I tell you, among those born of woman none is greater than John the Baptist" (Luke 7:28).

St Luke concludes the whole of John's message in one short, simple sentence:– "He preached good news to the people."

In his commentary on St Luke's gospel, Origen writes:

"For myself I think that the mystery of John is still being fulfilled in the world even today".

Wherever the values of the world are called in question in the light of the values of the Kingdom; wherever a fearless stand is taken against the evils of injustice and immorality; wherever men and women are prepared to face martyrdom rather than betray their integrity; wherever prophets, however great or popular, point beyond themselves to the Lord whose servants they are, there once again we hear the voice of John the lionheart calling us to behold the Lamb of God.

———————— * ————————

This twentieth century has seen more Christian martyrs than any other, and Guatemala has been the grave of many of them. Priests, pastors, catechists, lay Christians were all among the victims of the massacres that took place between 1980 and 1984. Up in the north-western part of the country some four hundred villages were razed to the ground, many of them centres of small Methodist communities. Their crime in the eyes of the authorities was that they were places where people were coming together in an organized way, reading their Bible, singing their hymns, but becoming dangerously subversive in their demands for social justice. It was feared that they might become a base for revolutionary uprising. So they must be silenced through systematic plans of liquidation.

Martyrdom literally means "witness", and the witness of these faithful followers of Christ has lived on in those who continue to work among the communities of the people called "Primitive Methodists". Their strength severely depleted in numbers, it has abated not at all in spirit. We were privileged to be the guests of this gallant Christian community for a few days as we travelled with one of their lay workers through the northern part of the country. Our visit began in the Church's modest headquarters, a house in a side street. The office wall was adorned with a diploma registering not some academic achievement of its occupier, but the gratitude of a labour organization working to provide better water supplies for the people. It seemed a good symbol for a Church to be identified with supplies of fresh water in a thirsty land. Throughout our conversation in the office, the phone rang insistently, calls from the many orphanages the Church now administers, from the weaving projects among the widows, from the feeding centres and the clinics – all Christian witness expressed through practical signs of the Kingdom.

One of the leaders gave his own testimony to his Christian conversion. It had not been, to use Methodist terminology, a "heart-warming" experience, but rather a heart-chilling one. He had been trained as a lawyer and was committed both to the conservative theology of his church and to the political discipline taught by the Government. But then in one of the villages he saw three hundred people rounded up in a chapel and killed in cold blood. One of the ministers of his church told him that he must not question what those in political authority had to do, and quoted to him the teaching in Romans 13. But he underwent what he called "a second conversion". He became convinced that the Church has to find a prophetic voice, a voice that both announces the Kingdom, the hope of the living Christ, and denounces the Government for its sins against the people. It must never allow itself to be silenced through fear. He knew himself what fear could mean. He confessed that there had been many times when he had feared for his life but he clearly had the fearlessness of faith and, in every sense of the word, the courage of conviction.

From that faithful little community we went on to visit another fearless prophet – one living in a bishop's residence, but without the fine raiment that was once associated with such palaces. The one luxury this bishop had was a video-cassette player, for which we were especially grateful as he could show us film of the courageous journey he had made only the day before, up into the mountains. He had gone there in answer to a call from a group of Indian families who had been living in hiding for the past five years, but who were now running out of food, and many of them were sick. They were afraid of being forced down by the military and being compelled to go and live in so-called "model villages" where they could be more strictly controlled and where they would be set to work on building roads in exchange for food.

This particular Catholic bishop was known to be a friend of the Indian people. He had worked among them and spoke their language. They trusted him and so had turned to him in their distress. Only if he would come personally and assure them that he would give them sanctuary would they consent to leave their hideout and come down into the town.

So we watched as the bishop climbed up to the appointed place, marked by a white plastic flag flying from a tree in the forest. Then at a signal, in single file, this uncertain band came out into the daylight, as timid as forest animals emerging out of shelter to seek food. Even the children tiptoed, for they had learned in the five years of hiding to move quietly and not to laugh or cry, lest their presence in the forest be detected. At last they were all out in the open, the sick among them being carried on makeshift stretchers. They followed the man of God to the waiting convoy of jeeps that drove them to the city and all the perils of "civilization".

Having seen the video recording of this cavalcade,

we were invited by the Bishop to go with him to the cathedral where the people were now being housed along the passage ways of an old, disused convent. They had had their first good meal for many months, had been kitted out with clothes, and were having their names registered. One girl who had been carried down on a chair because she had a gangrenous foot was seated on the floor, her foot now cleaned up and bandaged but obviously still very painful. Her husband sat beside her, looking on in mute compassion. Still nervous about what lay ahead, the people quietly joined us and the Bishop in a prayer of thanksgiving, grateful that for the time being at any rate they were in safe keeping.

Jesus did not only say, "Among those born of women none is greater than John". He went on to say, "Yet he who is least in the Kingdom of God is greater than he". For, as the Lord will say in the final judgement, "Whatsoever you do unto one of the least of these you have done it unto Me".

———————— * ————————

The Sanctus from the Campesino Mass

From all the roads,
paths and dells,
I glimpse Jesus Christ,
the light of your truth.
You are three times holy,
You are three times just,
Deliver us from the yoke,
Give us freedom.

You are the partner God,
You don't beat about the bush.
You are the just man,
the very head man.
You are three times holy,
You are three times just.
Deliver us from the yoke,
Give us freedom.

Translation by Liv Sovik

We light this third Advent candle to commemorate John the Baptist, prophet and martyr, who came out of the wilderness to bear witness to the light; and we pray for the peoples of Central America, that across the mountains and hills of those lands the voice of the prophets may be heard and the people rejoice in the coming of the Kingdom.

Collect for the Third Sunday in Advent

Almighty God,
who sent Your servant John the Baptist
to prepare Your people for the coming of Your
    son:
inspire the ministers and stewards of Your truth
to turn our disobedient hearts to the law of love;
that when He comes again in glory,
we may stand with confidence before before Him
    as our judge;
who is alive and reigns with You and the Holy
    Spirit,
one God, now and for ever.

Advent Four

And four for Mother Mary.
"I cannot see the way,
But You promise me a baby.
I believe You, I obey."

MARY

I once spent several hours in the BBC gramo-
phone library searching for a suitable setting of the
Magnificat – suitable, that is, for a programme I was
producing on the theme of motherhood. I wanted to
find music that would express the exultation of a
young woman on first learning the news that she is to
become a mother. Mary's song at the Annunciation
seemed an obvious choice. But then I encountered a
difficulty that had never occurred to me before.
Among the hundreds of recordings made of what must
be the most frequently sung of all the canticles, it was
almost impossible to find a recording of a solo
woman's voice singing it. Apart from one or two
operatic versions, almost every solo recording had the
ethereal, innocent ring of a choirboy's treble. What I
was looking for was the human quality of a woman's
warm emotion.

That led me to realize just how unearthly and unreal
the image of Mary and the import of her song have
become. Mother of God she may be, but for many

women she has lost a human face. A Roman Catholic priest emphasized the point for me when I heard him preach about Mary. He described how he had been trying to select a suitable actress to play the role in the annual nativity play. Almost instinctively he had sought out the quietest, most pious, most submissive-looking girl he could find. Then he asked her to learn the lines of the Magnificat. She whispered them demurely in her usual diffident manner, and he suddenly saw how inappropriate his casting was. For a song such as this he needed a strong, assertive woman, independent of mind and courageous of heart – the sort of woman he would be more likely to find, as he put it, in the Anti-Apartheid movement than in the Altar Guild. For this pre-eminently is the story of a courageous woman, and her song is one of liberation.

The Magnificat is clearly based on an earlier Jewish song which is found in 1 Samuel 2. There the singer is also a woman, Hannah, of whose strength of character and independence of action we are left in no doubt. Even her husband knows better than to overrule her decisions. She reacts angrily to the injustice in her own household where her childlessness is mocked by her more fortunate rival. So it is a song of judgement and of fulfilment that she sings when finally her prayers are answered. It is not surprising that it is these words that come to Mary's lips when she knows that she too is to bear a son. Maternity is for her, as it is for most women, the supreme gift, the magnifying of her womanhood. But it is more than that. It is the sign of God's choice of those who are in the world's eyes the lowest people, the weakest, the poorest, the

ones of no repute, but who are to become the vehicles
of God's grace, the agents of His salvation.

In our television series of "Songs of Praise for Advent"
we included in each programme a version of the
Magnificat sung in whatever style and setting seemed
appropriate within that particular culture. The one I
remember most clearly was the one sung for the Fourth
Sunday in Advent in our programme from Canada.
We had chosen as the location for the recording a large
church in the centre of Vancouver, the church of St
Andrew-Wesley, a gaunt, grey building with a square
tower and a long nave. It was well filled for the
occasion, with congregation and choirs gathered
mainly from the prosperous suburbs of that spectac-
ular city. They paraded in a fine array of fashions
and hair styles. The church building had been
attractively decorated with seasonal adornments,
displaying the skills of Canadian craft work. Gilded
angels, made of wire and gauze, floated over our
heads, quilted tapestries of nativity scenes hung on
the walls, poinsettias and evergreen glowed from
pedestal vases. In the stalls a blue-robed choir,
with professional precision, led the singing as the
church rang with the familiar carol, sung at breath-
catching speed, "Angels from the realms of glory".
Then came the quieter, haunting music of a Huron
carol, written by the martyr-missionary Father Jean
de Brébeuf in the language of the native Indian

people, and set to the tune of a tribal chant.

It was time then for the Magnificat. Lauren, a young teenager, dressed simply in a uniform grey pinafore dress and white blouse, her hair cropped in tomboy style, came to the front to lead the solo, a metrical setting of the canticle written by D. T. Niles and set to music by the Canadian composer Keith Bissell. She looked young and vulnerable in that splendid ecclesiastical setting. I wondered at first whether she was not too young for such a key role in the proceedings. Then I realized that she was probably about the same age as Mary of Nazareth had been when she first came on to the centre stage of the gospel story. As soon as Lauren began to sing I recognized that quality of voice and confidence of purpose I had been looking for. Here was no wilting, tremulous girl, but a young woman who, amazed that she had been chosen for such an important role, fulfilled it with every fibre of her being:

> My soul doth magnify the Lord; my spirit doth rejoice
> In God my Saviour, for His word declared to me His choice
> Of His handmaiden to become the mother of the Christ
> That for the Son of God my home and humble heart sufficed.

Lauren wants to be a professional singer when she grows up, but that is still a long way ahead, with high school graduation and four years at University and special training in voice production all to look forward to. Just coming into adolescence she is already enjoying the first stirrings of independence. In a country where women have now achieved almost total equality with men, she has a world of opportunity opening up to her and she seems like the kind of person who will grasp each opportunity with eager expectancy. For her, life is still full of fun and newly entered freedom. I asked her how she thought Mary must have felt when, at her age, she was told what God expected of her. "Scared, I guess," she said, "but proud too – a bit like I felt when I was asked to sing tonight. One part of me said 'Yes' straightaway, but the rest was real scary. I felt everyone was depending on me and I just had to stand here on my own and give it all I'd got."

That seemed not a bad way to approach the singing of the Magnificat.

References to Mary the mother of Jesus are surprisingly few in the biblical record, in contrast to the volumes of poems and prayers and books of devotion she has inspired down the centuries. In St Matthew's gospel she plays an almost entirely passive role in the nativity story. St Mark presents her as a mere onlooker at the ministry of Jesus. St John gives us a more intimate but complex picture of her relationship with her son at the marriage feast in Cana and at the foot of the Cross of Calvary. It is to St Luke's account, which has been called "the women's gospel", that we have to look for the fuller story of that maternal love which accepted the Christ into her womb, stayed with Him from the cradle to the cross, and was still among His faithful company in the early Church as they awaited the Pentecostal gift of the Holy Spirit. She is above all an "Advent person", the expectant mother, the anxious parent, the faithful disciple, the woman of prayer. Much of her life seems to be spent in waiting, and her words are few. But when she does speak, her utterances come from the heart. In her relationship with God her response is that of a woman of profound faith, glad to fulfil her mysterious vocation: "Behold the handmaid of the Lord; be it unto me according to Thy will." In her relationship with her son she expresses the ambivalent emotions of a mother torn between the pain and the pride of loving Him: "Son, why have you treated me so? Your father and I have been looking for you anxiously." "Son, they have no wine . . . Do whatever He tells you."

The tiny cameos we are given of Mary in the gospel stories have been turned into tapestries of legends woven around her in other writings. The apocryphal gospel of St James tells us that she was the daughter of Anna and Joachim, and that on her third birthday she was brought to the Temple and entrusted to the care of the priests. There, the story goes, she spun the scarlet thread for the Temple veil. At twelve years old she was betrothed to Joseph, a man of David's lineage. Tradition has it that she died in Ephesus, in the company of the apostle John, to whose care Jesus had commended her from the Cross.

Some have suggested that Mary is the "woman

clothed with the sun, with the moon under her feet, and on her head a crown of twelve stars", who appears in the Revelation of St John (Revelation 12:1-6). Countless mystics have seen her in their visions. She is reverenced in many faiths. In the Koran there are thirty-four references to her, far more than in the New Testament, and it is to Islam that we owe the preservation of the shrines associated with her, such as the Church of the Nativity in Bethlehem. In Hindu statuary there are representations of her among the gods and godesses. The earliest mention of the Christian story in China, which appears on an eighth-century tablet, states briefly "A virgin bore a sage". This young peasant woman has clearly captivated the religious heart of the world. Some have claimed that she represents the lost mother every human soul is seeking, who will intercede for her children and be the channel of mercy to them; some see her as the model woman of virtue and purity set on a pedestal of male fantasy, an impossible ideal for other women to emulate; some claim her as the first truly liberated woman, able to make her own choices and to hail the advent of one who comes to set all people free; some see her primarily as Mother of God, enthroned in splendour like His, to be venerated with awe and wonder; some even see her as the survival of a primitive goddess, redressing the balance in an all-male deity.

But who was she, this mysterious woman? And where did she really come from? Even St Matthew, who is so conscientious about tracing Jesus back to the House of David, details His ancestry through Joseph's line, with Mary appearing abruptly at the end, apparently disconnected with the rest of the genealogy. He does not seem concerned about who Mary's progenitors were, even though his narrative suggests that he accepted the tradition that she was a virgin when Jesus was conceived. The stupendous assertion that the humanity of Jesus must have been inherited from his female parent does not seem to have disturbed Matthew's confident assumption that it is the male line of descent that is important, even though he does include in this particular genealogy the names of three other remarkable women – Tamar, Rahab and Ruth, whose stories had helped to shape the history of the Jewish people.

But of Mary's history we know nothing, except that she was a woman chosen of God to shape in her womb the One who was to change the history of the world.

It was in Canada that I learned how much people long to know the history of their own descent and what has gone into the shaping of their lives. I have met families who have compiled strict genealogical records, tracing their line as far back as they can go, back beyond the pioneer days or beyond the years of indentured labour, to their lands of origin in Western and Eastern Europe, in Asia and in Africa. The only people who seem relaxed about where they come from are the ones rooted in the land, the native Canadians whose histories are kept alive in the oral legends of the past.

It is they who convey a strong sense of the community of the ancestors as well as of the living ones. Through shared stories of yesterday they keep alive the wisdom they need for survival today.

During a women's conference I attended in Toronto, I became conscious of how little most of us know about our own fore-mothers. Our fore-fathers are recalled for us in our family names, but the stories of the women in our history are lost beyond a generation or two. This came home to me in an evening ritual we held at an inter-faith conference attended by women from many different cultures and lands. In an act of worship we were invited to celebrate the communion of saints by each recalling the name of our mother, our grandmother and as far back as we could go through our maternal line. Most of us were unable to go back more than two generations. "I am Pauline, daughter of Daisy, daughter of Lucy, daughter of a woman whose name I do not know but who came from a village in Oxfordshire" – "I am Heidi, daughter of Ursula, daughter of Helga, who emigrated to Canada from Germany" – "I am Rachel, daughter of Sara, daughter of a woman who died in a concentration camp in Poland" – "I am Shirley, daughter of Hilda, daughter of Betsy, daughter of a slave of African descent" – "I am Mary, daughter of Mai-Ling, daughter of a Chinese woman who came to join her husband working on the Canadian Pacific railway."

We realized as we shared our histories how inter-twined all our lives were, as the descendants of those who had set out freely from Europe to seek a new life in Canada now stood next to the granddaughters of those who had been compelled to come here by slavery or starvation.

The stories of some of those pioneer women were poignant and yet inspiring, reminding us of the courage and the kindness women can show towards one another. A Canadian told the story of one of those extraordinary women who braved the hardships of a cruel Canadian winter to accompany their husbands on the long trek westwards, setting up their home-steads on the way. This woman and her husband had built their own earth and timber hut on the plains of Alberta, where one winter he had to leave her alone with their four-year-old daughter whilst he went off to Edmonton to work on the railroad. When he returned the following Spring he found that his little girl had died of flu, but he had two more twin daughters, born while the mother was alone and isolated. She had gone into labour as the child lay dying. Agonizing in childbirth, she was unable to send for help. She could only watch her daughter die. Then there was a knock on the door. An Indian squaw was standing there, though they were strangers to one another. "I noticed no smoke coming from your chimney," she said, "and wondered whether anything was wrong." She took away the dead child for burial and came back to help with the delivery of the new babies, wrapping them round in furs to keep them warm, and comforting the mother as best she could.

Small wonder that such a story has stayed alive in the family memory. The women who have attended to the needs of the birthing and the dying are the women who hold in their hands the love that has shaped our lives.

We are not told whether Mary had a midwife at the birth in Bethlehem, but it would seem more than likely that some woman from the inn, or a companion on that long eighty-five mile journey from Nazareth to Bethlehem would have come to her help. Yet, like so many women who must have played a part in the gospel stories, her presence is not recorded for us. At least we know that Mary had prepared well for her son's birth. She had the swaddling clothes there to wrap around Him, and had made ready a place for Him to lay His head. The pangs of childbirth were, as she was soon to discover, only the first of the pains her love for Him would cause throughout the rest of her life. The sword that had seemed to pierce her side then would pierce it again when she saw the sword plunged into His side on the cross. And between the birth and the death there was a long lesson of learning how to let go of Him whom she sometimes seems to have loved "not wisely but too well".

In the Western tradition of Christianity, Mary's humanity is stressed in the representations of her in Christian art, in the titles accorded to her by the faithful, and in the prayers offered through her name in intercession. She is the Madonna who suckles her child and smiles at Him, she is the woman to whom "Love gave a thousand names", as Edward Schillebeeckx puts it in his book *Mary, Mother of the Redemption*. But love has a way of using exaggerated language, and some of the titles in later centuries seem to take us further and further away from the simple girl of Bethlehem. She becomes "The Star" of storm-tossed seamen, the "Aqueduct of God's grace", the "Queen of Heaven", the "Mother of Mercy".

Yet Jesus seems to have denied her even the name of Mother. "Woman, what have you to do with me?" He asks her when she seeks help from Him on behalf of the embarrassed host at the wedding in Cana. "My hour is not yet come."

"Who is my mother?" He asks, when told that she has come the two-day journey to Capernaum to find Him during his preaching mission. "Whoever does the will of my Father in heaven is my brother and sister and mother." Even in His dying moment on the Cross, as He commits her to the care of John, He again addresses her as "Woman", saying, "Behold your son. Son, behold your mother". It is as though He sees her not simply as His mother but as a woman who needs to let go of her bonds to Him, as He needs to let go of His bonds to her. The birth is not complete until the cord is severed and both child and mother are free.

That is a hard lesson for any mother to learn, one that takes a lifetime of listening and loving and letting go. But Mary learns it, even as she stays near her son, so often keeping silent vigil, but pondering in her heart all that He says and does. When He shows His first sign of independence and leaves her worrying about His coming home late she lets Him know of her concern, but she tries to understand too as He speaks words of wisdom whose depths she cannot plumb. She swallows her hurt pride when she sees Him dishonoured as a prophet in His own country. She follows at a distance along the road she is certain will lead Him to danger and death in Jerusalem. She waits with the other women to lift His body from the cross. There is nothing supernatural or sentimental about this kind of mother love. It is the maturing of a motherhood that can let the other be.

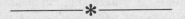

In Canada I often heard people express a concern about the language we use in addressing God. There is a great awareness throughout North America of the prevalence of sexist overtones in the use of our language in most areas of discourse. We tend to suggest by our constant choice of male pronouns or masculine generic terms that the male is the norm and the female the deviation. People have become conscious of this in the Church as in all other spheres of life, and there have been widespread attempts to rid the language of hymnody, of liturgy and even of the Scriptures of a predominant male bias. I understand the concern. Language, however symbolic, reinforces concepts which can then become set in concrete. I have often told the story of a Sunday School class I was once teaching about the story of Mary and how she prepared for the birth of Jesus, making the swaddling clothes and attending to the crib. A little boy asked innocently, "Why didn't God send the baby with his clothes already on?" Whereupon a little girl peremptorily replied, "Don't be silly, God's a man. He can't knit!" I admired her feminine pride but despaired of her theology. Yet I could understand it. All the images she had ever heard of God the "Father in heaven", the "King of Kings", the "Lord Almighty" had conjured up for her a clear picture of a powerful male being who, in her experience, would still be dependent upon the female to take care of all the practical details of life.

So I found it interesting in Canada to hear preachers frequently trying to correct the imbalance by using the term "Mother God". There are certainly hints of its admissibility in some scriptural passages, but it would seem that it has different connotations for women than it has for men. Mother tends to be for her daughters the less indulgent parent. She expects them to grow up and take responsibility even if she continues to coddle her sons. So for women "come of age" the concept of the Motherhood of God might well be a more appropriate one. But for men, it would seem that the reverse is generally true. The concept of God's motherhood may still have clinging to it traces of the stranglehold which mother love can sometimes imply, which may be one reason why Jesus Himself never used the term in addressing God. It suggests to me that both terms are necessary if our relationship to God is to be a fully rounded one.

But when, through the cult of the Virgin Mother, that maternal love has been put upon the pedestal of an idealism so far beyond any real woman's reach – for

no woman on earth can be both virgin and mother –
then maybe the word itself needs a certain liberation
before we can confidently employ it to describe our
liberating God.

At the Vancouver School of Theology, where I was
privileged to spend a term in residence, I heard of a
course of remarkable meditations that had been given
there recently by Maria Teresa Porcile, a Catholic
theologian from Uruguay. She had spoken of Mary
the mother of Jesus as a "paradigm of liberation". She
had called her the "open" one, who opened not only
her womb but her heart also to the Word of God. She
is the one who takes the Incarnate Word both into the
Temple and out into the world. She is, as it were, both
priest and prophet, the first to receive the Holy Spirit
within her inner being and the first to be impelled by
that Spirit to share the joy of her Lord as she
proclaims the new order He has come to inaugurate.
Her words reminded me of the great Marian hymn of
the Greek Orthodox Church which hails Mary as
"Space of the spaceless God, Gate of the sublime
mystery".

It was refreshing to meet in Canada women now
able to fulfil their vocations as both priests and
prophets. At the seminary over half the students
preparing for either the Anglican priesthood or the
ministry of the United Church are women. Hearing
them preach and watching them celebrate the Sacra-
ments I was moved by the way in which they so
naturally and easily use their experiences as women to
communicate their faith, discovering in the Scriptures
truths that have lain hidden from men's eyes. To

understand the fullness of faith we need both masculine and feminine insights. We need those who can become, as it were, midwives of Christ in a world travailing to bring to birth the faith and the hope and the love of the daughters and sons of God.

St John is the only one of the gospel writers to make any reference to Mary's vigil at the Cross, but the image of the mother sharing her son's suffering right up to the last bitter agony has so imprinted itself upon human memory that it has inspired some of our greatest art and statuary, music and poetry. The figure standing silently before the Cross became, in developing legend, one of the main participants in the whole drama of the Passion. At the time of the crusades, pilgrims to the Holy Land imagined the sorrowing mother accompanying her son, as they traced His steps along the Via Dolorosa. For those unable to make the pilgrimage, the Stations of the Cross represented in sculpture or painting Mary's meeting with Jesus on the way to Calvary, staunching His wounds and finally taking His dead body into her arms and helping to prepare Him for His burial. Among the world's greatest statues is Michelangelo's Pieta, where even cold stone seems to become warm with compassion as the grieving Mary holds once again in her arms the body of the son she bore, now bearing His sorrows as her own.

The cult of the Mother of Sorrows flowered

particularly in the Middle Ages, when in the grief brought by plague and early death, many turned for consolation to the one whom they saw as sharing their anguish. Poems expressing Mary's imagined lament and even her bitter questioning at the death of her son became part of the Good Friday re-enactment of the Passion story. In her book, *Alone of All Her Sex*, Marina Warner quotes one of the earliest and most beautiful of such laments, a poem written in the thirteenth century by the Italian poet Jacopone da Todi, a lawyer who became a Franciscan friar, one of those known as "God's minstrels". In his poem *Lady of Paradise* he imagines a dialogue between Jesus and Mary, as she stands at the foot of the cross. He asks:

> "Mamma, why have you come?
> You cause me a mortal wound,
> For your weeping pierces me
> And seems to me the sharpest sword."

And she responds:

> "Son, white and ruddy,
> Son without compare
> Son, on whom shall I rely?
> Son, have you also forsaken me?"

Son, why? The question Mary asks is the question many a woman has cried out in her suffering, not only to Mary's son, but, like Him, to God Himself. Why have you forsaken me? And the answer comes only through one who stands close by, to wipe the tears, to kiss away the pain, to surround us with the everlasting arms of love.

Yet to some women it seems that even God has forsaken them when through His Church they have been made to feel unworthy of handling sacred things, as though they were tainted by their own sexuality. The Mary who is pictured as caressing in her own arms the broken body of her son would still in many parts of the Church not be allowed to consecrate the elements of that body in the Holy Eucharist.

Today, Mary has become for many women the one who stands with and for and beside them in their sorrows, and opposes with them all that would diminish rather than magnify their sex. She is the one who proclaims that the hungry are to be filled with good things, she is the one who begs wine for the thirsty, she is the one who gives birth to the living and buries the dead. She is the one who holds, as it were, the margins between this life and the next. She is the one who dares to say her own Yes to God and to stand in solidarity with all who open their lives to both the joys and the sorrows of love.

One of the first studies ever commissioned by the World Council of Churches at its founding in 1948 was on the Role and Status of Women in the Church. It was a study that prompted a widespread response from women all over the world. In the years immediately following the Second World War, women were becoming increasingly active in public life, working alongside male colleagues in rebuilding broken communities, rehousing refugees, re-opening channels for peace-making and reconciliation. The report had many recommendations to make as to how the churches could more effectively recruit and train women for new forms of ministry and greater participation in the life of the Church.

The report received scant attention at the first Assembly of the World Council which, like most policy-making bodies, was at that time composed almost entirely of men. But a special Department was set up, later to be known as the Co-operation of Women and Men in Church and Society. From that desk ever since, pressure has been exerted to encourage churches throughout the world to make fuller use of the talents and energy of women.

During the United Nations Decade of Women (1975-1985) worldwide attention was directed to ways in which women are discriminated against in all areas of life – in education, in economic resources, in career opportunities, even, in some parts of the world, in the provision of basic amenities. The World Council of Churches helped to highlight these issues and launched its own study on the "Community of Women and Men" which involved more local groups in ecumenical action and theological reflection than any other of its programmes. Encouraged by such a response and aware of how wide-ranging were the concerns expressed through it, the Central Committee of the WCC called for a further "Ecumenical Decade of Churches in Solidarity with Women" to begin in 1988.

Initially there was an outcry against the suggestion

that to mark the inauguration of the Decade women should be invited to preach on Easter Sunday. Some pastors felt it to be an outrageous idea that women should take over the pulpits at this major feast of the Church. The Scripture readings for that day might well have reminded them that the first preachers of the Resurrection were the women who came to the tomb of the risen Lord, though the gospels record that even their words were dismissed by the men as idle tales!

In Vancouver, the Decade of Churches in Solidarity with Women began on a wet Sunday evening in September 1988. It was the kind of evening which would deter all but enthusiasts from stirring from the comfort of an armchair to venture out into the pouring rain and on to the hard pews. But the group of women who had planned this "Liturgy to Begin", as they called it, were indeed enthusiasts and had managed to spread the infection of their enthusiasm to a large company of people. Some came out of curiosity as to what this cumbersome title was meant to imply and what they were letting themselves in for over the next ten years. Some came full of scepticism that the churches ever would overcome the monstrous sexism that for so long has marred Christian witness and alienated many young feminists from the faith. But many came hoping that this would mark the beginning of a new partnership in the Gospel, in which men and women together could explore what it means to share the one new humanity in Christ.

In the Presbyterian chapel where the service was held there were posters and photographs reminding us that the people in Canada were being invited to share not just a North American concern about women's equality, but to express solidarity with women the world over, for many of whom life is a constant struggle against exploitation and deprivation. In the poverty-stricken lands of the world it is the women who bear the heaviest burdens as they try to feed their hungry children, care for the frail elderly, farm parched land, market undervalued produce.

There were reminders in the church too of the creativity of women who, even out of the necessities of life, make things of great beauty. There were embroidered cloths from India, batik wall hangings from Indonesia, and quilted bedclothes from Canada. It was a Canadian poet who wrote of the pioneer women:

We had to make quilts to keep our children warm.
We had to make them beautiful to keep our souls
    alive.

The liturgy for the service had been drawn up by a group of women belonging to different churches, Protestant, Anglican and Catholic, who together had pooled materials and written their own prayers. In doing so they had been made aware that their common experience as women was a deeper unifying force than their denominational separation. At the start of the service four symbols were presented, suggesting the common elements of creation, things which are part of women's daily life but which have themselves become symbols of the holy things too: bread and water, fire and incense.

Lesley, who had been one of the group responsible for preparing the service, told me afterwards that she had grave doubts as to how seriously the churches would take this concern to highlight for the next ten years the so-called "women's issues". So often, she said, they are set aside as peripheral or sentimental. But, she vehemently emphasized, the issues with which women are concerned are literally issues of life and death, and they are sentimental only if by that is meant that they are matters of the heart as well as of the head.

Lesley could hear in Mary's "Magnificat" a song that has an authentic ring for every woman who has known in early pregnancy the feeling that this coming child will bring new hope into the world, that this child will have some special vocation. As the child grows within her, the outward exultation turns to an inward anxiety about matters of the immediate moment. How shall I feed this child? How shall I know what is best for a tiny infant totally dependent upon me? So much of a mother's life, said Lesley, herself the mother of five sons, is spent "pondering" on the welfare of her children and providing for the need of others.

But that can never be the whole of life for any woman. We all have our own journey to make. "My own mother died of cancer", she said, "and we spent a lot of time together, for we were not only mother and daughter but best friends as well. In those last weeks, when she knew the end was near, she said to me, "You can't possibly understand where I am now. There is a great space between us, but stay with me to the end."

———————— * ————————

In Psalm 51 the Hebrew word used to describe the loving-kindness of God literally means the feeling a mother has for the child of her womb, a mercy that enfolds us all the days of our life and meets us even beyond the tomb. It is the compassion that feels with and for others, the solidarity which means that no one is ever entirely alone. Through life and death, from generation to generation we are all accompanied and liberated by the loving-mercy of God. He that is mighty has magnified us.

Ah, Mary we hardly know you

Ah, Mary we hardly know you —

A few tantalizing glimpses

    relegated by most to "introduction"
    useful to lead into the "real" story,
    relegated to the task and place of women —
        standing by and watching over,
        caring for needs,
        keeping a death watch,
        providing loving care
            for the body of the dead one,
            the child of your womb.

Ah, Mary we discover you —

One who was open and receptive —

    open to the love and mercy of God,
    open to embodiment of the living word,
        receptive to life,
        you became filled with life.

Ah, Mary you have become the glory of God –

"The glory of God is a human being fully alive."
You are the glory of God!

Ah, Mary you have become the dwelling place of God –

a God of liberating power,
the power of love.

Ah, Mary we hardly know you –

A few tantalizing glimpses
but we look at you afresh
and in you we begin to see ourselves.

We are the dwelling place of God,

We are the glory of God.
Thanks be to God!

Taken from verses written by Karen Summers,
Vancouver School of Theology, 1987

We light the fourth Advent candle for Mary the mother
of Jesus, and pray for women the world over that, like
her, they may have courage to say "Yes" to God and
to a life of liberating love.

106

Collect for the Fourth Sunday in Advent

Heavenly Father,
who chose the Virgin Mary, full of grace,
to be the mother of our Lord and Saviour:
fill us with Your grace,
that in all things we may accept Your holy will,
and with her rejoice in Your salvation:
through Jesus Christ our Lord.

Christmas Day

And Christ is in the centre,
For this is His birthday,
With the shining lights of Christmas
Singing: "He has come today."

GOOD NEWS FOR ALL PEOPLE

No one knows the exact date of Jesus' birthday. The first mention of 25th December as the day Jesus was born in Bethlehem was in a calendar of civil and religious events compiled in Rome in AD 345. This date was chosen probably because it was the day for celebrating the mid-winter festival, the "birth of the unconquered sun". It may have been a move to counteract the influence of the pagan feasts that were popular throughout the northern hemisphere at that time of the year; it may have had a profounder meaning. Towards the end of the second century an anonymous Christian writer, commenting on the festival of the mid-winter solstice, wrote:

They call [this day] "the birth of the unconquered sun". But is the sun so unconquered as our Lord Who underwent death and overcame it? Or they say it is "the birthday of the sun". But is our Lord

108

not the Sun of Righteousness of Whom the prophet said: "For you who fear my name, the sun of righteousness shall rise, with healing in its wings."

B. Botte, *Les origines de Noel*, p 105

It became one of the great themes of the Christmas celebration that not simply human beings, but the whole creation rejoiced together at the birth of Jesus. "Let all creation dance and thrill with joy, for Christ has come to call it home and to save our souls", sings a processional antiphon in the Byzantine liturgy for the feast of Christmas. And in one of the sermons of St Maximus of Turin, he writes,

> The people are quite right, in a way, when they call this birthday of the Lord "the new Sun" . . . We gladly accept the name, because at the coming of the Saviour not only is mankind saved, but the very light of the sun is renewed.
>
> Sermo 621 Corpus Christianorum, Series Latina 23:261

This linking of Christmas with the winter festival meant that for Christians in the northern hemisphere the images of light and darkness, of glory shining from the heavens, became strong metaphors for all that the coming of Jesus means, expressing and enlarging the concept of the cosmic Christ, in Whom the whole creation is held together. It meant too that many of the customs associated with the pagan festivals were taken over into the Christian celebrations, so that people could go on enjoying their feasting on the fat of the land, adorning their homes with evergreens, burning their Yule logs, and, as we have observed during

Advent, lighting their candles on laurel wreaths. Thus they sanctified the pagan culture rather than destroying it.

It would seem that those early Christian messengers were wiser than later missionaries who, so often in the name of the Gospel, felt the need to obliterate all traces of old tradition lest it contaminate in some way the purity of the new faith. Yet it was to share all our lives that Christ came, to a particular place at a particular time, so that all places and all times might know Him and celebrate His coming.

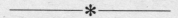

One place where they have no need to dream of a white Christmas, because it is almost inevitable, is Kisbiox, a village five hundred miles from Vancouver, the home of the Git-Ksan people, among the mountains of British Columbia. It was there that we found our Christmas baby. She was the daughter of a Native Indian family who had taken part in our Advent Songs of Praise from Vancouver. When we were invited up to the home of one of the chiefs of the Wolf tribe and were told that there would be a new-born baby there, we decided straightaway that she would be the baby to feature in our Christmas Day programme.

On our flight up from Vancouver to Terrace, the nearest airport to Kisbiox, but still a long day's road journey away, we speculated about the kind of customs that might surround the birth of a child in the Native Indian tradition (with an eye, of course, to some good television shots!). Perhaps she would be wrapped in a specially bright blanket, with smoke signals announcing her arrival and a ceremony to give her a name as tinkling in sound as the rivers that meet at the foot of the mountains where she lives. When we arrived, our illusions were immediately dispelled. Little Hilary was fashionably dressed in a nylon romper suit, her grandmother was informed of her birth by telephone, and one of her first toys was a Cabbage Patch doll! So, has this Indian family lost all trace of their inheritance of native tradition?

Not at all. In fact, one of the good things being celebrated just at that time in Kisbiox was the taking down of a fence that had literally once divided the "Christians" from the "pagans" in the village – a relic of the days now past when those wanting to embrace the faith of Christ had been encouraged to sever all connections with the customs of their unconverted neighbours.

Of recent years the United Church of Canada has repented of this destruction of another people's culture, and its leaders have publicly sought forgiveness from the Native Indians for all the damage that was done, not only in negating a rich cultural inheritance but thereby almost robbing a people of their identity. That apology, the chief told us, had brought great rejoicing. The Moderator of the Church described how he had taken the written apology from the Church's conference to a great tepee, the tent where the Indian elders had gathered. There he knelt down by the fire and on his knees read out to the assembled company the words of penitence. Following the reading there was a long silence, and then one aged Indian woman said, "I have waited all my life to hear someone say those words, not only for my own sake, but for my children and grandchildren!" Then, wrapping both arms around the church leader in a warm embrace, she declared, "Of course we forgive you".

So, despite the Western trappings of so much that we saw in that Indian home, we were to discover too how deeply the people still ponder in their hearts and treasure in their lives the wisdom of their ancestors, and how eagerly now they are rediscovering the traditions of the feast-hall, and rejoicing in the totem poles which for so long have stood like sentinels guarding the village. Baby Hilary will indeed learn the ways of the tribe, when she receives her first Indian name, according to custom, at the age of five, and again when she receives another name to mark her puberty, and again another name as she comes into the status of a married woman. Each period of her life will be celebrated in native style as she grows up, affirmed as a member of a proud and ancient community.

"What will you name your child?" is the question we all ask a new mother. Mary would have replied with the name the angel told her to give him, "Jesus – the one who sets all people free", and with the name the prophets had foretold, "Immanuel – God with us."

---- * ----

I have only ever seen an angel once. It was on a rainy day, when I was eight years old. I had been kept indoors all morning, but at last the clouds cleared a little, the rain stopped and I went out to play. No one was about, so I filled the time waiting for my friends by throwing a ball up against the side of the house. Then I looked up and saw the angel – high above me, robed in white, haloed in gold and floating across a sky that had suddenly cleared to a violet blue. I ran to call my mother to come and see my angel. She was busy and had no time to come just at that moment, but she said, "You are very lucky to see that angel. Not many people see them. I expect if I came I would see only a cloud, edged with sunshine in a rainy sky. But you have seen an angel." "What is an angel?" I asked her. "It really means a messenger of God," she said, "and God sends messages to us in many ways. Your angel is telling you what a beautiful place the world can be, even on a rainy day."

Angels come in many shapes and sizes, but they all bring messages. In the biblical stories, the messages often begin with the same words: "Do not be afraid!" It is like an answering chorus to the first words Adam spoke to God when he was discovered hiding in the Garden of Eden: "I was afraid." In the darkness of night, out on the hillside near Bethlehem, the shepherds saw their angel. "Be not afraid", came the message. "Behold, I bring you good news of a great joy which will come to all the people – for to you is born this day in the city of David a Saviour, who is Christ the Lord."

It was to simple people that the angels appeared

first. The simpler we are, the younger we are, the clearer is our vision. And it was to a simple place that the angel sent them. In his book, *The Gospel in Solentiname* Ernesto Cardenal records how a group of peasants discussing the shepherd's story commented that if Jesus had been born in a rich house the shepherds would probably never have been let in. In any case they would not have wanted to go there because it would have seemed as though it had nothing to do with them. What happens in the houses of the rich is no good news for the poor. But the angel said this was good news, of great joy, for all people. So they decided this included them and they went to see for themselves.

There they found the babe, wrapped in swaddling clothes, lying in the manger. And they went home and told everyone about it. That is all there is to the story of the shepherds. Yet for over thirteen centuries, ever since the story was first dramatized in the Christmas liturgy in Jerusalem in AD 635, their experience has been re-enacted in countless nativity plays. It has grown in the telling of it, as the shepherds have taken on characters of their own, the angels have multiplied in number, and choirs of carol singers across the world have bidden us to hear the herald angels sing, "Glory to the new-born King".

One five-year-old West Indian friend of mine, delighted to be cast as the chief angel in her school nativity play, was rehearsing with me the words she had to say. So I asked her to tell me the whole story of what happened in Bethlehem. With the bright-eyed excitement of a child she painted the picture for me in vivid detail. I listened attentively until suddenly she stopped and asked, "Haven't you ever heard this story before?" "Not like you tell it", I answered her. Christmas is a story told anew in every generation.

"Good news of great joy for all people", announced the angel. There is nothing quite like spending Christmas among people for whom this story really is news, people who have only recently heard it for the first time. That was how it was for the Khongsai people in Burma, whom I was privileged to visit once just at Christmas time to share in celebrations which were still a new occasion for them. Only a few years before they had moved down from Assam, where they were finding it difficult to grow enough food, to settle in the more fertile area of the Somra Tract in Upper Burma. There, in clearings they had hacked out of the jungle, they had planted rice and were able to grow fruits and vegetables. So they had built homes for themselves and, influenced by a missionary family who had gone to live among them, had built also a church, a school room and a football pitch – an interesting provision for body, mind and spirit!

To reach this village of Maingdaungphai, my companion, Florence Cleaver, and I had to travel for a whole week in a river-boat chugging up the River Chindwin, past rafts and canoes and sampans, steering a zigzag course to avoid sandbanks on either side of the water. With us on our journey were David and

Maureen Turtle, an Irish missionary family taking their two children and two-week-old baby back to their home in the Somra Tract. We spent our travelling days watching the changing scenes of river life in the fishing villages coming down to the water's edge, sometimes glimpsing the vivid colours of tropical birds flashing through the forests, observing water buffalo bathing in the river or admiring the slender pagodas, like wedding cake decorations, crowning the ridged hilltops. We docked for the nights at quiet harbour towns where we were graciously welcomed by stall-holders in the market places, who offered us refreshment. The river steamer took us as far as Homalin, but we still had further to travel upstream by small motor boat.

When, five days before Christmas, we arrived at our destination, Maingdaungphai, our reception was tumultuous. "They've come! They've come!" shouted one group after another as they scrambled down the river bank to meet us. The centre of attention was the new baby Simon, who was passed up from one pair of arms to another as he was carried in triumphant procession to the home already decorated to receive him. There was no Christmas tree or snow scene. There was no point in dreaming of a white Christmas here. But there was a star and a crib and a card on which someone had painstakingly written "Happy Birthday, Jesus".

But the holiday had not yet begun. The next day I was taken by the local minister, Haolet, to see the people at work in the *taungya*, the rice cultivation. There co-operatively they were harvesting the crop in the area of jungle they had cleared together and sown together. The women were bringing the cut rice, in great bundles fastened on their backs, to a bamboo mat where the men were threshing it with long, three-pronged forks, which beat out the ears of rice from the straw. These they winnowed by flapping cloths and kicking the rice into the centre. Finally, the precious grain was carried to a store made of bamboo, in a temporary shelter, from which they would carry it as needed back into the village. Haolet not only preached the parables about winnowing and harvesting, he also shared in the work of it with the people.

Maureen Turtle was quickly back at work too. She was a doctor and her principal concern at the dispensary she ran in Maingdaungphai was the treatment of trachoma, an eye-disease endemic in this river area. The treatment is comparatively simple given the right ointment and skilled medical attention, but for many people it was as though miracles of healing were happening as those threatened with blindness were able to open their eyes and see again. No wonder the crowds quickly gathered at the dispensary now that she had returned. They called her "the woman who makes people see".

David and I were told that we had a special invitation to go the next day to a village some miles further into the jungle where the people were preparing for their first Christmas. A young teacher had been going there from Maingdaungphai to teach them the Christmas story. Florence would stay with the children at home, and David and I would be accompanied by Hope Musgrave, another missionary who was training teachers to serve that whole area of the Somra Tract. So we set off, again by motor-boat, and then a four-mile trek through the jungle to the newly settled village of Khelseibung.

As we pushed our way through the dense bamboo and paddled across the muddy streams, I felt as though I had strayed into an old war film by mistake, and kept expecting a sniper's bullet to come whizzing past my ears. But instead I was in for an even greater surprise. For suddenly my ears were assailed by a strangely familiar sound. Above the chattering of monkeys I could hear the singing of a Christmas carol. At first the words were quite indistinguishable. But the tune was unmistakable – it was "Once in royal David's city stood a lowly cattle shed".

Suddenly we saw where the sound was coming from. We emerged from the jungle into an open clearing where a few bamboo and timber-built sheds perched up on poles formed the village of Khelseibung. And right in the centre of the clearing was a specially erected arch of bamboo and palm, complete with a scarlet and white curtain drawn to hide from our view the little group of children who had gathered to welcome us. With great ceremony we were bidden to sit down on the stools provided for us soft-living people from the West, while the curtain was drawn back to reveal the choir, who sang the story of Christmas to us, told in a few simple lyrics, a story quite new to them. Some of them had been Christians for only six months. Yet in many ways the story was closer to their lives than to ours.

I realized how close it was the next morning. We

stayed for the night in the largest of those bamboo homes, having a hilarious party together with our hosts before we lay down to rest in our sleeping bags on the rough boards of the floor. The Khongsais had danced some of their own folk dances for us, and we – the two missionaries and I – had tried to return the compliment, though our repertoire was limited to the Irish jig, the Sailor's Hornpipe and the Gay Gordons, which quite literally nearly brought the house down. Then the Christmas party had ended with the prayer these people had learned especially for the occasion, the prayer Jesus had bidden all people to pray, as together we called on God, our Father.

But the differences in our lives within this one family of God were brought home to me with a shock the next morning. A neighbour came into the house we were in. "Come quickly", she pleaded. "My sister's baby is just about to be born and we need your help." None of us were medical workers – David was a minister, Hope a teacher and I was nothing at all of any use in a situation like that. But Hope and I were almost pushed into the house to attend to the young fifteen-year-old who was quite obviously dangerously ill and frightened too. This was no normal birth. The youngster needed skilled medical attention urgently. But what could we do? The nearest help was Maureen back in Maingdaungphai. She was the only doctor for a hundred miles upriver. To get the girl to her dispensary would mean someone carrying the patient all those miles through the jungle along which we had trekked and then back on the motor-boat. It seemed unlikely that she was strong enough to stand the hazards of such travelling. So Hope set about doing what she could. "Don't be afraid", she said to the girl. "We are here to help you."

"We'll keep her as clean as possible", she said to me. "Fetch me hot water and cotton wool if you can find any." I asked desperately for hot water, but the only pot in the house contained rice beer, and the water would have to be fetched from the muddy stream we'd paddled through. I searched for cotton wool but all I had were the twists in the top of a couple of aspirin bottles. David produced a small first aid box with a packet of gauze in it. Somehow Hope made the girl clean and comfortable, despite the dogs and rats and piglets who scrabbled about over the floor on which she was lying. Clearly someone would have to stay with her, at least until the danger was past. So Hope agreed to stay, while David and I made our way back to Maingdaungphai to seek Maureen's advice as to what else we could do.

"There's only one thing worse than being in your situation not knowing what to do," said Maureen, "and that is to be in my situation knowing what ought to be done but having too few resources to do it. You have done all you could. We can only pray that somehow the girl will pull through despite everything." So we prayed and waited for Hope's return next day, after her long night's vigil and her battle to save a young life. When she did get back she had her thumbs up. The girl was alive and doing well, though the baby was lost. It had never had a chance to survive.

It was Christmas Eve when Hope came back to us,

and the people in the village of Maingdaungphai were preparing for their great festivities. The children from the school were practising their nativity play; the shepherds, not having any lambs, had brought a mongrel dog; the kings' crowns were made of cardboard; there was a great silver star carried by a tall angel; Mary and Joseph were of miniature size. Yet somehow they conveyed the sheer wonder that it was in a world of need and poverty and despair that God allowed His Son to be born. And because I had just seen what such need and poverty and despair could mean in that lowly shed where a mother had lost her baby, I shared the wonder in a new way.

At four o'clock in the morning on Christmas Day I heard carol singers again. The youth group in Maingdaungphai were parading around the football pitch with colourful lanterns, calling all the faithful to hear the herald angels sing. As we gathered in the chapel, the dawn rose golden across the sky. There was a nip in the air, but there was magic, too. The people came, wrapped in their woven blankets, looking like biblical characters themselves. I watched them bringing their Christmas gifts and placing them on the Communion Table – boxes of matches and a few candles, handfuls of rice and bowls of eggs, fruits and vegetables, their rich gifts to the One Who had come to share their poverty, gifts to share with all the community.

Then came the feasting – venison brought in from the forest, and rice and vegetables grown in the jungle clearing. As we gathered round the fire where the food had been cooked the story-telling began. It was the young people who were telling the story, whilst the elders listened with rapt attention. "Good news of great joy to all people", announced the angel. The audience laughed and clapped, delighted especially when the juvenile shepherds tumbled over each other as they went running, as gleefully as the actors in a mediaeval mystery play, to see the new-born child. And there he lay on a bale of straw – not a doll, but a real, live human baby. It was Simon, the one who had been brought by his mother and father, messengers of good news who had come as "angels" to live among them and who had brought the promise of healing and hope to the people of the Somra Tract.

And the glory of the Lord shone round about them.

"In the beginning was the Word . . . and the Word was made flesh and dwelt among us and we beheld his glory, glory as of the only begotten of the Father, full of grace and truth."

Many and Great, O God, are Your works,
Maker of earth and sky,
Your hands have set the heavens with stars,
Your fingers spread the mountains and plains,
Lo, at Your word the waters were formed,
Deep seas obey Your voice.

Grant unto us communion with You,
O Star-abiding One,
With You are found the gifts of life.
Bless us with life that has no end,
Eternal life with You.

Dakota Hymn, North American
Indian Tradition

We light this Christmas candle for Jesus Christ, who
came to bring good news to us and to all people, and
we pray for all who have gone to announce the good
news to others and who celebrate His birthday with
them, as He comes, in many happy returns, to dwell
among us all today.

Collect for the Christmas Vigil

Eternal God,
who made this most holy night
to shine with the brightness of Your one true
light;
bring us, who have known the revelation of that
light on earth,
to see the radiance of Your heavenly glory;
through Jesus Christ our Lord.

BIBLIOGRAPHY

The following books may be helpful to anyone wanting to read further:

The Liturgical Year by Adrian Nount, OSB, The Order of St Benedict Inc., Collegeville, Minnesota, USA

Proclamation: Advent – Christmas by D. Walterudel and G. Kendal, Fortress Press, USA, 1973

Immanuel by Hans-Ruedi Weber, World Council of Churches

ACKNOWLEDGEMENTS

The author is grateful for permission to use the following material:

"The People's Creed" from *Gospel From the Ghetto* by the Rev. Canaan Banana, circulated by the Urban Mission Desk of the World Council of Churches, Geneva, 1973

The Sanctus from the Campesino Mass translated by Liv Sovik, Geneva

Verses written by Karen Summers called "Ah, Mary we hardly know you", during the Vancouver School of Theology, 1987

The Dakota hymn from *Songs for Gospel People* – the hymn book of the United Church of Canada.

Fount Paperbacks

Fount is one of the leading paperback publishers of religious books and below are some of its recent titles.

☐ FRIENDSHIP WITH GOD David Hope £2.95
☐ THE DARK FACE OF REALITY Martin Israel £2.95
☐ LIVING WITH CONTRADICTION Esther de Waal £2.95
☐ FROM EAST TO WEST Brigid Marlin £3.95
☐ GUIDE TO THE HERE AND HEREAFTER
                                       Lionel Blue/Jonathan Magonet £4.50
☐ CHRISTIAN ENGLAND (1 Vol) David Edwards £10.95
☐ MASTERING SADHANA Carlos Valles £3.95
☐ THE GREAT GOD ROBBERY George Carey £2.95
☐ CALLED TO ACTION Fran Beckett £2.95
☐ TENSIONS Harry Williams £2.50
☐ CONVERSION Malcolm Muggeridge £2.95
☐ INVISIBLE NETWORK Frank Wright £2.95
☐ THE DANCE OF LOVE Stephen Verney £3.95
☐ THANK YOU, PADRE Joan Clifford £2.50
☐ LIGHT AND LIFE Grazyna Sikorska £2.95
☐ CELEBRATION Margaret Spufford £2.95
☐ GOODNIGHT LORD Georgette Butcher £2.95
☐ GROWING OLDER Una Kroll £2.95

All Fount Paperbacks are available at your bookshop or newsagent, or they can be ordered by post from Fount Paperbacks, Cash Sales Department, G.P.O. Box 29, Douglas, Isle of Man. Please send purchase price plus 22p per book, maximum postage £3. Customers outside the UK send purchase price, plus 22p per book. Cheque, postal order or money order. No currency.

NAME (Block letters) _____

ADDRESS_____

_____

_____

While every effort is made to keep prices low, it is sometimes necessary to increase them at short notice. Fount Paperbacks reserve the right to show new retail prices on covers which may differ from those previously advertised in the text or elsewhere.